... STORY OF RADAR

PLATE I

SOME SENIOR MEN OF T.R.E.

R. A. SMITH   R. C. COCKBURN

J. A. RATCLIFFE   C. HOLT SMITH   THE AUTHOR   W. B. LEWIS

P. I. Dee and D. Taylor were not present when the photograph was taken

ONE STORY OF RADAR

BY

A. P. ROWE

C.B.E.

CAMBRIDGE

AT THE UNIVERSITY PRESS

1948

621.384

CAMBRIDGE
UNIVERSITY PRESS

University Printing House, Cambridge CB2 8BS, United Kingdom

Cambridge University Press is part of the University of Cambridge.

It furthers the University's mission by disseminating knowledge in the pursuit of education, learning and research at the highest international levels of excellence.

www.cambridge.org
Information on this title: www.cambridge.org/9781107494794

First published 1948
First paperback edition 2015

A catalogue record for this publication is available from the British Library

ISBN 978-1-107-49479-4 Paperback

CONTENTS

CONTENTS

ILLUSTRATIONS

FOREWORD

MARSHAL OF THE R.A.F. LORD TEDDER

THE scientist, the technician and the Service user are, and must be, a united team if our defence is to keep up to date. That is the text, and the moral, of this book. Moreover, a defence that is out of date is no defence.

There are some nowadays who say that, in this scientific age, the scientist should be the master in defence matters: I have yet to meet a scientist with knowledge of defence problems who would subscribe to that view. There are others who say that the scientist should be kept in his place as a servant of the Defence Services: if the Services in general, and the Royal Air Force in particular, had adopted that attitude from 1935 onward the Story of Radar—and of the war—would have been tragically different from what it was.

I was fortunate in having considerable dealings in 1938–40 with the 'Boffins' (as the Royal Air Force affectionately dubbed the scientists), and will never forget the invigorating atmosphere that pervaded Bawdsey and, later, Worth Matravers. Here was brilliant individualism harnessed to make a great team without loss of individual freedom and initiative. This freedom of individual thought was given its full expression in those stimulating weekly conferences which, with the paradoxical humour which is so typical of our people, were called 'Sunday Soviets'. That, in my view, was the outstanding achievement and was the real secret of success—the creation of a real team without losing the vital spark of individual freedom. It is perhaps because this type of teamwork is of the very essence of the Royal Air Force that such happy relations were established between the Service and our friends and partners, the Boffins. On the other hand, let it never be forgotten that such a team spirit might well never have been created had it not been for men like Rowe and Tizard who could and did interpret the user to the scientist and the scientist to the user. They, and men like them, set a pattern which is not only vital for our future security, but may well, I suggest, be vital for the well-being of the world.

1948

PREFACE

I SUPPOSE that many who write a first book without thought of writing another feel an urge to touch their readers upon the shoulder and say, 'Wait a moment. I know I have been guilty of writing a book but, before you read it, I want to explain why I wrote it and what it is about.'

Certainly there are some things I want to say to a potential reader and I will set them out in as tidy a fashion as I can:

(*a*) This is not the story of radar, which is a gigantic task for the official historians to undertake. It is no more than one man's story of one Experimental Establishment belonging to one Government Department. It is one story of the Telecommunications Research Establishment, better known as T.R.E., which worked upon radar and allied problems, first under the Air Ministry and then under the Ministry of Aircraft Production. The story concerns the period from June 1934 to September 1945.

(*b*) I have written this book in Australia during a short break in my working life. The sources of information at my disposal have been statements on radar issued to the press by the Ministry of Aircraft Production, some factual material, chiefly relating to dates and ranks of Service personnel, collected for me by Ivor Worsfold, and my memory. Had my purpose been to write a history of T.R.E., these sources would have been hopelessly inadequate, but it is possible that the sparsity of the records at my disposal has helped me to concentrate upon the only aspect of T.R.E. about which I have felt an urge to write. My main purpose has been to provide the general reader with a description of how one Government Research

Establishment went about its business, what it was trying to do and how far it succeeded. It is not uncommon for young scientists, and older ones too, to believe that scientific adventure and freedom to explore new ground can be found in Universities but not in Government Establishments working for the defence Services. In this story I have provided material enabling the reader to judge whether we lacked adventures or the freedom to pursue them.

(c) This paragraph is written for those readers who knew T.R.E. and who may seek and fail to find reference to many things and to many people. The omissions are explained by my belief that to complicate the story unnecessarily would defeat the purpose I have defined. I have not forgotten that we worked for the Royal Navy as well as for the Royal Air Force, though to a much smaller extent. I have not forgotten the many successful projects which find no place in my story nor that grand work was done in the laboratories and hangars at the aerodromes which served us, as well as at the main Establishment. Least of all have I forgotten that vast majority of my some-time colleagues whose names are unrecorded in this book. They will remember that we used to pride ourselves on our singleness of purpose. It is this principle that has led me to simplify my story, to avoid making a catalogue of T.R.E. devices and to omit names unless they have arisen naturally in the course of the story. I think they will understand.

(d) The question of origins is often a thorny one in scientific work, but for the radar devices evolved by T.R.E. I do not find it troublesome. The yardstick I have adopted in my story is a simple and consistent one. We were working in a field of applied science and I have taken the time of birth of a device to be when members of a team first took off their coats, built equipment and demonstrated its practicability. On this basis I have ignored any British claim to the origin of radar prior to 1935, when Watson-Watt and his team demonstrated the practicability of the floodlighting system used in the Battle of Britain. On the same basis, other T.R.E. teams can claim the origin of, for example, the Plan Position Indicator and the Ground-Controlled Interception set in 1940, Gee in 1940–41 and H_2S late in 1941. I have no personal knowledge of whether other countries demonstrated the practicability of radar before 1935, but I have never met an American scientist who did not give the British full credit for the birth, in 1940, of the era of centimetre radar. I have however tried to avoid the common error of exaggerating the importance of 'first-times'.

In making public the story of T.R.E. only one matter troubles me. It is that the pattern of our lives in war should be thought worthy, in large measure, of the days of peace. The magnitude of our belief in our contribution to survival and the objectivity which pervaded the Establishment often made us intolerant of those whose ways were not our ways and of those who seemed unable to keep pace. The struggles of a drowning man to reach the shore may make a story, and some of the qualities he brings to the fight for survival are not to be despised when the shore is reached. Yet I believe that those who gave most to T.R.E. have no wish that the ruthless objectivity of our war days should be followed in time of peace, nor that life should be a constant struggle for mere survival.

(e) I acknowledge with great gratitude the indispensable secretarial help given me by Miss Dulcie Finck of Adelaide and the labours of my wife who enacted the part of a highly critical member of the general public. As I write this preface, I cannot forecast the ultimate extent of my debt to Ivor Worsfold, but it will be heavy for he has accepted the task of receiving the manuscript and seeing it through its pre-publication stages.

(*f*) I have not been asked to write this book by any Government Department. On the other hand, it is an indication of the freedom enjoyed by a Professional Civil Servant that no Government Department has hindered its publication. I must stress, however, that the opinions expressed are my own and are not necessarily held by any Government Department.

A. P. R.

ADELAIDE
SOUTH AUSTRALIA

February 1947

CHAPTER I

THE BEGINNING

FOR ME, the beginning was in June 1934. It is perhaps typical of that period that I was the only member of the Headquarters' staff of the Director of Scientific Research, Air Ministry, employed wholly on armament problems and the legality of even this meagre contribution was open to doubt. It is odd to reflect that when H. E. Wimperis was appointed in 1924 as the first Director of Scientific Research at the Air Ministry, it was decided that armament, airships and radio were not his concern. Science in relation to the weapons of war has travelled far since then. In the 1914–18 war, great contributions had been made by individual scientists serving the Royal Air Force and particularly by H. T. Tizard, F. A. Lindemann and B. Melvill Jones, but an integration of military and scientific thought had to await for its birth the coming of another and more dangerous war.

Lest it should happen again, it is well to note some of the reasons why much of the armament research work of the 1920's, and most of the 1930's, was poor in comparison with, for example, progress in aeronautics and in power units for aircraft. Very few scientists could be attracted in time of peace to work on armament problems and, even had they been available, the money for their salaries and their experiments would have been difficult to find. In those days, armament research work was almost wholly controlled by competent and conscientious R.A.F. officers who concentrated upon improving the weapons familiar to them. Thus there was little scope for the civilian scientist in armament work. Perhaps above all there was the curse of secrecy. Although secrecy in defence science is often essential and although no man of good will would break a pledge of secrecy, it must be admitted that the more secret a project the less efficient it is likely to be. The science of aeronautics, for instance, progressed rapidly under a system of healthy competition between the Royal Aircraft Establishment at Farnborough and the National Physical Laboratory at Teddington, whereas knowledge of armament work was known only to the few engaged upon it and workers in this field rarely, if ever, had to encounter the criticism of greater or even other minds.

It is therefore not surprising that the conception of the technique of bombing accepted in those days bore hardly any relation to the methods eventually used by Bomber Command in its devastation of Germany. For day bombing, highly optimistic figures for accuracy were obtained by methods rarely appropriate to war. Proposals for night bombing were something of a mystery; navigation and target identification being difficult at night, it was proposed that the target area should be illuminated by a preceding aircraft so that following aircraft could see the target. How the first aircraft could find the target in order to illuminate it was not explained.

If some were anxious about armament progress, few lost any sleep. Was there not an edict, comforting to the uneasy and a strength to those who hesitated to spend money, which read, 'No war for ten years'? I doubt if the original Cabinet directive was as definite as these five costly words but there is no doubt that the attitude towards armament work was dominated by them. Almost, it seemed, they were written over the door of every office.

I have said that, for me, the beginning was in June 1934 because it was then that I began to wonder, from my small corner, whether our air-defence arrangements were healthier than air armament. Hitler was firmly established and already 'No war for ten years' was losing its comfortable ring. Certainly the little I knew of preparations for air defence gave small comfort. The big problem was of course to counter mass air raids by day against our industrial targets. Even in 1934 it was appreciated that this was a task for fighter aircraft and that anti-aircraft guns, however useful in lowering enemy morale and raising that of the civil population under attack, could not be expected to destroy an effective percentage of the attacking aircraft. But how were the fighter aircraft to be in the right place at the right time, i.e. how were they to intercept the enemy before he could drop his bombs on important targets? In theory, one answer was known as 'standing patrols'. At all times when weather and other conditions made air attack likely, or even possible, squadrons of fighter aircraft would patrol the skies in wait for the enemy's approaches to probable targets. It was however only a theory and it is doubtful whether any one believed in its practicability; even had we, at the time of the Battle of Britain, owned every fighter aircraft in the world they would hardly have sufficed. Thus the importance of an early warning of the approach of hostile aircraft along observed tracks had been clearly recognized in the 1920's, and it was hoped that the range of location would suffice to enable the patrolling fighter aircraft to be directed to the most effective positions for attacking the oncoming bombers.

Already by 1934, research on early warning had been for many years conducted by the War Office but the hopes vested in this work seem pathetic now. Let us for a moment look forward six years to the Battle of Britain, in which radar tracked enemy aircraft at ranges of 50 and often 100 miles from our coasts and frequently observed the enemy circling his aerodromes while forming up for the attack. Let us remember the exceptionally fine weather of that fearful summer of 1940 which made attack at all times likely and remember that, even with radar, the fighter aircraft available to us only just sufficed. Remembering these things, it will readily be seen that standing patrols, even if assisted by a few minutes' warning, would have been hopelessly inadequate. Some genius has said that victory goes to the side that gets most sleep. It was radar that enabled our pilots to rest and our mechanics to get their aircraft ready for battle, until it was known that the enemy was approaching.

The War Office research on early warning was directed towards the use of special equipment for listening to approaching enemy aircraft. Two huge concrete mirrors, 200 ft. in length, were erected on our coast and, for all I know, may still be there. In spite of painstaking research on the part of an able team of scientists under W. S. Tucker, the warning given by these means would rarely have exceeded two or three minutes and the truth of the matter is that this unpromising work went on because there was apparently no other hope. I remember well the depression which invariably came over me after witnessing the efforts of these scientists to get blood out of a stone.

In June 1934, then, against a background of frustration in armament work and gloom over the War Office work on early warning of air attack, I undertook an informal survey of the problem of air defence and to this end collected every available file on the subject; there were fifty-three of them. It was clear that the Air Staff had given conscientious thought and effort to the design of fighter aircraft, to methods of using them without early warning and to balloon defences. It was also clear however that little or no effort had been made to call on science to find

4

a way out. I therefore wrote a memorandum summarizing the unhappy position and proposing that the Director of Scientific Research should tell the Secretary of State for Air of the dangers ahead. The memorandum said that unless science evolved some new method of aiding air defence, we were likely to lose the next war if it started within ten years. Unfortunately, I was not clever enough to think of a new method.

I have described the state of air defence as I knew it in 1934. For me there was no more peace of mind, and I recall that my holiday companion of that year had to listen to gloomy predictions regarding the coming war. That a few others were equally worried, I have no doubt; but whatever their worries or mine, there was no sign in that summer of a drive to solve the problems of air defence.

The turning point came in November 1934. Wimperis, as Director of Scientific Research, had seen clearly that no solution was likely to be forthcoming without scientific aid from outside the Air Ministry. A true integration of scientific and military thought was as yet unborn, and a lesser man might have struggled to solve the problem with the few men and tools at his disposal.

Wimperis, who sowed much that others reaped, took a bold step, the results of which neither he nor anyone else could have wholly expected; a step without which defeat might have come instead of victory. He proposed the setting up of a committee, to be called the Committee for the Scientific Survey of Air Defence, under the chairmanship of H. T. Tizard. The members were to be P. M. S. Blackett, A. V. Hill, and H. E. Wimperis as the only Air Ministry member, with myself as Secretary. These proposals were accepted and an astonishing change came over the whole scene. I shall not easily forget how, under the forceful personality of its chairman, the committee brought

5

a sense of purpose and growing achievement to all it touched.

It was at this time that radar was born, though in a form which bore no more relation to the final product than a new-born babe bears to a full-grown man. This is how it happened. Whilst making his final preparations for the new Tizard Committee, Wimperis wrote to the Superintendent of the Radio Department of the National Physical Laboratory, R. A. Watson-Watt, on the possibilities of a 'death ray'.

For many years the 'death ray' had been a hardy annual among optimistic inventors. The usual claim was that by means of a ray emanating from a secret device (known to us in the Air Ministry as a Black Box) the inventor had killed rabbits at short distances and if only he were given time and money, particularly money, he would produce a bigger and better ray which would destroy any object, such as an aircraft, on to which the ray was directed. Inventors were diffident about discussing the contents of their black boxes and, despite the protection afforded by the patent laws, invariably wanted some of the taxpayers' money before there could be any discussion of their ideas. The Ministry solved the problem by offering £1,000 to any owner of a Black Box who could demonstrate the killing of a sheep at a range of 100 yards, the secret to remain with its owner.

The mortality rate of sheep was not affected by this offer. The idea of a death ray however was not absurd and something of the kind may come within a hundred years. Because of the recurring claims regarding such rays, there is little doubt that, in writing to Watson-Watt, Wimperis hoped to dispose of the problem, one way or the other, before the Tizard Committee met; the problem being whether it was possible to concentrate in an electromagnetic beam sufficient energy to melt the metal structure of an aircraft or incapacitate the crew. Watson-Watt's answer to Wimperis's death-ray question was a simple one. He said that, although there was no possibility of directing enough energy on to an aircraft to produce a lethal effect at useful distances, it should be possible to locate the plan position of an aircraft by measuring its distances from two points on the ground. The principle was simple enough. Every schoolboy knows that he can measure his distance from a cliff by timing the interval between his shout and the reception of the echo from the cliff. Watson-Watt proposed that a pulse or 'shout' of electromagnetic energy (which travels at about 186,000 miles per second) should be emitted from a point on the ground so as to be incident on an aircraft which, he calculated, would reflect or reradiate back sufficient energy to enable an 'echo' to be received. He pointed out that the tiny fraction of a second between sending out a pulse and receiving an echo could be measured on a cathode-ray oscillograph, an instrument which later became familiar to tens of thousands of men and women in the armed forces. The principle involved was not new. E. V. Appleton and others had by this method measured distances from electrically charged layers in the atmosphere and had located the positions of thunderstorms by obtaining reflections from electrically charged clouds. In practice, they sent out not one 'shout' or pulse but a succession at extremely short intervals and so obtained a continuous record on a cathode-ray oscillograph of the distance of the reflecting object from the source of the emitted energy.

Wimperis immediately detected a sign of hope in Watson-Watt's suggestion and asked him to prepare a paper for the first meeting of the Tizard Committee. This was held in January 1935. Realizing that calculations were not enough, the committee wanted the earliest possible practical demonstration that Watson-Watt's proposals were worth pursuing; they wanted a demonstration of what scientists call an 'effect'. Watson-Watt therefore proposed that an aircraft should fly in the 50-metre Daventry radio beam used for Empire broadcasting and that he should erect simple equipment on the ground to demonstrate whether sufficient energy was reflected from the aircraft to produce an 'effect' with his instruments.

This was done near Daventry on 26 February 1935. Graphic accounts have been written of this demonstration, of how senior officers from the fighting Services went to Daventry on that great day; how for the first time the position of an aircraft was obtained by radar and how success was hailed with congratulations from the distinguished onlookers. In fact, none of these things happened. Though there was not a demonstration of the location of an aircraft, what happened was significant enough. Overnight one of Watson-Watt's assistants, A. F. Wilkins, had erected equipment in a van near Daventry. All that was hoped of this equipment was that it would show that an aircraft, when in the Daventry beam, would reflect enough of the beam's energy for its presence somewhere in the vicinity to be inferred from observations in the van. This is just what happened on 26 February 1935. So far from the demonstration being witnessed by distinguished officers from the Services, the sole representative from the Service departments was one humble civilian scientific worker—myself. Watson-Watt and I were pleased with the demonstration, since reflections from the aircraft were obtained when it was estimated to be about eight miles away, but we knew that we had not seen the location of an aircraft by radio.

I reported favourably to the Tizard Committee. From now on, there was no hesitation on the part of the committee and soon this story will move more and more to the laboratories. The embryo of T.R.E. which eventually grew to 3,000 men and women was about to be formed and steps were to be taken which largely initiated the growth of the radio industry to a war figure exceeding £100,000,000 annually.

This is the moment to pause and to consider why radar was born in the spring of 1935 instead of earlier or later, and perhaps the moment to pay tribute to the pioneers. Those who do not move in scientific circles are inclined to think of inventors as men who, like Archimedes, spring from their baths shouting 'Eureka' when some great truth is vouchsafed them. The public and therefore the press usually demand that the name of one man shall be heralded as the inventor; it is simpler for all concerned. Few important advances in applied science happen in this way and certainly radar did not. The first experiments on radar could have been started at least two years earlier than they were, for the technique used by Appleton, Watson-Watt and others for measuring the distances of electrically charged layers in the upper atmosphere was known years before the birth of radar. For what then was the beginning of radar waiting? It awaited contact between those with a need and those with a technique which could meet that need; contact between Wimperis seeking means to improve our defences and Watson-Watt who was engaged on a technique without thought of a military application. Again and again throughout this story we shall see the vital need for contact between the man with a need and the man with a technique. To any who claim to have originated radar before the spring of 1935 there is but one answer: 'Why did you do nothing about it?' Certainly no whisper of the possibility of locating aircraft by radio means reached the Air Ministry before the described events occurred.

Radar was not an invention, like a zip-fastener; yet I see little difficulty in naming the British workers who were chiefly responsible for the momentous events of 1935. Appleton and his colleagues had already evolved a new technique without thought of its application to defence. Wimperis inspired the formation of the Tizard Committee, made the first contact with Watson-Watt and saw the potentialities of his proposals, and persuaded him to throw in his lot with the Air Ministry. That grand body, the Tizard Committee, provided a degree of objectivity and driving power which it has not been my fortune to see equalled in the work of any other committee. But more than to any of these, credit for the first radar successes belongs to Watson-Watt; not for suggesting aircraft location when approached by Wimperis, because any one of half a dozen workers might have given the same answer; not even for invention, because ideas of greater novelty and ingenuity were to come later from those as yet unheard of in the radar field; but for having such faith in his proposals that he gladly left his work at the National Physical Laboratory and staked his scientific reputation on success, with no more grounds than a few calculations and a sketchy experiment. From the earliest days, Watson-Watt had no doubt that a vast new field in applied science had been opened.

Soon my story will move closer to the laboratories from whence were to come other pioneers in the ever-expanding field of radar.

CHAPTER II

LONDON AND ORFORDNESS

I N February 1935 we find the Director of Scientific Research at the Air Ministry, backed by a powerful advisory body of independent scientists, in possession of an idea which might overcome the chief obstacle to successful defence against hostile aircraft, i.e. that of getting fighter aircraft to the right place at the right time.

An idea, however, is but a beginning and what had next to be done was clear to all concerned. Approval for scientific work to begin had to be obtained from the Member of the Air Council for Supply and Research (then Air Marshal Sir Hugh Dowding); this meant that money had to be obtained for experiments at a time when money for research on defending our country was hard to come by. Scientific staff experienced in the appropriate technique and willing to work on defence problems had to be found and a site for the work had to be chosen which fulfilled many conditions, not least of which was an isolation from towns demanded by security considerations.

These then were the problems: money, men and a place in which to work. Let us see how these needs were met. Possessors of new ideas of apparent military value are often depicted as struggling for recognition against the stupidity and vested interests of Colonel Blimp and his opposite numbers in the other Services, and history is not without examples supporting this picture. It is therefore pleasant to record that authority for the first experiments on radar was immediately forthcoming. There were naturally those who thought the scheme unworkable (as indeed it was in its earliest form); but no important voice, Service or civilian, was heard to obstruct the proposal to set up a team of scientific men to make experiments and to try to demonstrate, for the first time, the location of aircraft by means of radio. It is easy now to regard as obvious the approval given by senior R.A.F. officers for experiments to begin, but to those of us who were aware of the financial stringency of those days there was nothing obvious about their support. All honour then to the Air Council which gave its support to radar when it was but an idea.

The next problem was to find the men for the first experiments and there was little doubt about where to look for them and no doubt about the choice of their leader. The Radio department of the National Physical Laboratory, under the Superintendentship of Watson-Watt, was the centre in this country of experiments on the location of electrically charged regions in the upper atmosphere. In Watson-Watt therefore was found a man who had played a part in evolving the necessary technique and who was not daunted by the vast scale of the effort needed to turn an idea into a working scheme for air defence. Thus it came about that he and a handful of his assistants were lent to the Air Ministry by the Department of Scientific and Industrial Research to make the first experiments.

There remained the problem of where to do the experiments. Technical considerations called for a flat area of land; a coastal site was needed to provide the realistic conditions of aircraft approaching our coasts over the sea; the need for speed demanded the immediate availability of electric power and laboratory space and the need for secrecy was paramount. A short digression on the highly controversial subject of secrecy in scientific work is perhaps permissible. The feeling among scientists that no scientific work should be secret is not new, but it was not until the use of the atomic bomb that the general public became aware of this feeling. For myself, I fail to see any difficulty in this matter. Scientific work of a fundamental character, done at Universities or elsewhere, should be unfettered by secrecy, but *applied* research for defence purposes must often be secret; that because of secrecy it will fail to attract some good men and will usually progress less rapidly than non-secret work is inevitable and must be accepted. From its beginning, radar was applied research and secrecy was of paramount importance because of its vital role in the defence of this country. Not until the Battle of Britain was well advanced was a radar station subjected to bombing; moreover the enemy failed to render the operation of radar stations difficult or impossible by jamming. What folly it would have been to publish the astonishing scientific progress which eventually meant so much to this country!

The site chosen for the first radar experiments was Orfordness, surely one of the loveliest places in the world. At Aldeburgh, in Suffolk, the River Ore flows to within a few yards of the sea and then fortunately turns south and flows for 11 miles, leaving an isthmus of singular beauty. To the many who loved it, and to the many more who did not, it was known as 'the Island' and those who first worked there on radar were known as 'the Islanders'. They were not, however, the first scientific men to work on the island. In 1935 Orfordness already had its aerodrome, its power supplies and its laboratories. During the 1914–18 war it had been used for armament research work, which was revived in 1929. During two summers in the early 1930's I had lived on Orfordness and so, from a London office, could envy the first radar workers who had a fascinating job to do among pink thrift and yellow shingle and the cries of the terns.

No time was lost in beginning work. The crude Daventry test which showed that electromagnetic energy reflected from an aircraft could give an observable effect on a ground instrument was held in February 1935. By 13 May of the same year a team had been assembled, Orfordness was ready for the work and special equipment had been constructed. On that day the Islanders began to instal their equipment and on 31 May it was ready for tests. The intimate story of those early days must be told by those who experienced at first hand the thrills of achievement. I was only a visitor, privileged to see the work whenever I could escape from London, but I well remember that though my body was in London, my heart was at Orfordness.

Results were not long in coming. On 15 June 1935, under bad conditions of radio reception, the Tizard Committee saw an aircraft followed by radar to a distance of 17 miles, its range from the observers being continuously measured. In July a range of 40 miles had been achieved. Forty miles! Here surely was hope at last; after years of work on sound location, ranges of about 10 miles were the most that could be got under average conditions but now a primitive form of radar was observing aircraft at 40 miles after only two months' work.

Before going further, let us be clear about the ultimate objectives of these early experiments and let us see how many of them were in sight of fulfilment and how many were not. To enable fighter aircraft to engage hostile bombers the following information was considered necessary:

(a) The approximate but continuous plan position of the oncoming bombers at the greatest possible ranges from our coasts; 50 miles was regarded as a great help and 100 miles as ample. A positional accuracy of two or three miles was considered adequate. Plan position could, in theory, be obtained either by measuring ranges alone from two or more spaced radar stations or by measuring the range and also the bearing of an aircraft from one radar station.

(*b*) The approximate height of the oncoming enemy bombers. Clearly it would delay, and perhaps render impossible, an interception if the fighters found themselves at the plan position of the enemy but two or three miles beneath them.

(*c*) The approximate strength of the hostile formations. If radar indications were the same for one aircraft as for a hundred, it would have been impossible for Fighter Command in the Battle of Britain to direct the few available fighters on to the strongest attacking formations.

(*d*) Whether an aircraft observed by radar was friend or foe. This factor was of greater importance in countering night bombing than it was, for example, in the Battle of Britain.

The above information, i.e. plan position, height, numbers and identification, was needed concerning hostile aircraft approaching any part of our coasts.

This book aims to use radar as an example of how scientific work for defence is done, to show how such work proceeds from step to step and to give some idea of the enormous gap, in terms of effort and money, between the first scientific experiment and full achievement. The magnitude of this gap is not always appreciated, particularly by scientists engaged on fundamental work, but it should be appreciated by the taxpayer.

In July 1935 all concerned were elated at the results obtained by a handful of scientists at Orfordness, but let us see, in relation to the needs defined above, how far they had really got.

One station at Orfordness could measure the range of an aircraft, or formation of aircraft, up to a distance of about 40 miles out to sea. To enable this to be done, a transmitting station 'illuminated' an area off the coast with electromagnetic energy (radio waves), the area being something like a circle to which the coast formed a tangent at the station. This illumination, or floodlighting, was done with the packets or pulses of energy characteristic of radar. An aircraft within the illuminated area reradiated some of the energy it received and a very small part of this reradiated energy was received at the Orfordness station. Provided the aircraft was within the attainable radar range, a continuous record of the distance of the aircraft from the Orfordness station was displayed on a cathode-ray oscillograph. In those early days it was intended that at least two neighbouring stations of a chain round our coasts should measure range only and so find position. No satisfactory way of measuring bearing seemed to be attainable at an early date.

Of the other wanted data, aircraft height had not been measured in July 1935 but an early success had been achieved with the counting of aircraft. On 24 July a formation of Hart aircraft was correctly recorded as consisting of three aircraft; a 'red letter' day. Approximate counting was possible because each of the aircraft reradiated some of the transmitted energy, and the combined effect of receiving the reradiated pulses from a formation of aircraft in characteristic motion gave a valuable clue to numbers. The remaining problem, that of distinguishing friend from foe, was not solved until 1939.

This was the position after two months of experimental work and further successes were soon to follow. By mid-September 1935 the height of an aircraft flying at 7,000 ft. was measured with an error of little more than 1,000 ft., which was good enough for interception; but the most far-reaching success of that late summer was the solution of direction finding which enabled plan position to be got from one radar station. I must confess that, from my London office, lack of direction finding had seemed a major stumbling-block to the use of radar for defence purposes, but the speed with which the problem was solved was typical of the period. On one of his visits to London, I remember confronting Watson-Watt with some sketches showing how difficult, and perhaps impossible, it would be to rely only on range measurements when several hostile aircraft or aircraft formations were scattered over the North Sea. Within a few days Watson-Watt was back with a solution, and I never again doubted that radar could solve the problem of interception.

By the autumn of 1935 it was clear that a cheap experiment performed by a handful of scientists had succeeded but that a practical defence scheme based on radar would cost a lot of money, money in terms of millions of pounds. The early results had been got with 70 ft. masts and it was known that the higher the aerial systems, the greater the ranges. It was known, too, that the cost of a mast increases rapidly with increase of height. A simple, fairly low-powered transmitter had been used at Orfordness but it was clear that far higher powers were needed, powers which research sponsored by the Admiralty had shown were attainable; moreover, to counter deliberate jamming, the transmitters were required to work on a number of wavelengths, with facilities for rapid switching from one to the other. Similar costly work was demanded for the receiving systems. But one radar station, however efficient and however intricate, would only begin to meet the needs of air defence. It was known that similar stations would need to be built at intervals round our coasts, particularly on the east and south coasts. Even with the erection of these stations, the end of the period of vast expenditure would not be in sight. The recording, at coastal radar stations, of the movements of incoming hostile aircraft would be of little use unless the information were sent rapidly to the users, i.e. to Fighter Command, to Group Headquarters and to the Fighter Stations where were based the aircraft which would have to intercept the enemy. All this would mean more costly equipment and large-scale laying of special lines of communication.

Success, then, seemed likely, but the price would have to be paid; a price which corresponded to that of a mere after-noon of a major war but a price which in 1935 seemed stupendous and one which was beyond the powers of the Air Ministry, or even of the Treasury, to approve without Cabinet authority. Fortunately, the mechanism for gaining Cabinet support was already available. In the spring of 1935 a sub-committee of the Committee of Imperial Defence had been set up, under the chairmanship of Lord Swinton, then Sir Philip Cunliffe-Lister, to deal with air-defence pro-blems, and it was to this committee that the Tizard Com-mittee appealed for funds and for general support on a large scale.

It does not now seem remarkable that a few members of the Government, some high ranking officers from the fighting Services, three or four scientists, the head of the Treasury and a few other prominent men should get to-gether round a table to discuss the defence of Great Britain against air attack, but in 1935 it was an event. As Joint Secretary with Wing-Commander John Hodsoll, I listened to the discussions of the committee with mixed feelings; but if some of its members had little to give, others gave much in their different fashions. In particular I recall the energy and quickness of mind of the Chairman, Sir Philip Cunliffe-Lister, to whom radar owes much; the wise watchfulness of Sir Maurice Hankey; the persistent urging of Mr Winston Churchill that *something* should be done, though he did not always understand the language of the scientists. I recall, too, how readily, after years of starvation of armament re-search, Treasury approval for large expenditures was signi-fied by a nod across the table from Sir Warren Fisher. In my experience the big men of the British Civil Service are nearly always ready to look at problems in a big way and to make big decisions. Frustrations usually arise from the cumulative effect of obstructions from smaller minds.

Those were great days. There was not always to be unanimity between the scientist, the Service user and the men with the money, but in 1935 the almost traditional obstructiveness which scientific men are supposed to meet was absent. The Tizard Committee believed in the future of radar and the Air Staff backed its belief with a degree of faith which at the time amounted to courage; and, not least, the money was forthcoming.

CHAPTER III

BAWDSEY

IT was not long before Orfordness began to suffer from growing pains, an affliction from which the Radar Research Establishment, however much it changed its name and place, was to suffer until relieved by a surgical operation appropriate to the peace of 1946. Approval had been given for the erection of a 240 ft. aerial tower at Orfordness. It served its purpose because in March 1936 a record range of 75 miles was achieved; but 240 ft. masts bordering aerodromes are not popular with airmen and the need to go elsewhere, for this and many other reasons, was soon apparent. Signs were not lacking that the handful of scientific staff would need to grow, though none could know that the research Establishment of which the Islanders were the embryo would eventually attain a strength of 3,000. A long vista of possibilities and probabilities stretched ahead, needing more and more scientists, with draughtsmen and skilled mechanics to support them; needing men and women to do administrative and clerical work, to be responsible for stores, to guard the Establishment against intruders, to clean the laboratories and to do a hundred other tasks inseparable from applied research and development. These men and women needed somewhere to work and somewhere to live, amenities which few places in England were less likely to provide than Orfordness and its surroundings.

Somehow a compromise had to be found between a degree of isolation demanded by technical and security considerations and proximity to the commonly accepted blessings of civilization. A solution was soon found, in which a glass of ginger beer played its part. About 20 miles south of Orfordness, at the mouth of the River Deben, was an isolated estate of about 250 acres belonging to Sir Cuthbert Quilter and known as Bawdsey Manor. The Manor house was large enough to provide the laboratory space then needed and to provide a home for some of the scientists. The grounds were spacious enough for experimental work and for the construction of what eventually was to be the first of the chain of radar stations guarding our coasts. Across the ferry at the mouth of the Deben was the terminus of a bus service to Felixstowe, where the bulk of the staff were soon to live.

During the late summer of 1935 I accompanied my chief, Wimperis, on an informal inspection of the outside of the estate. Like two conspirators we studied the Manor from the beach and between the hedges. But was there any possibility of acquiring the property? The days of requisitioning were yet to come. It was clear that a little local gossip would help, and where better to seek it than at a ginger-beer stall near the entrance to the coveted estate? There were rumours, it seemed, that Sir Cuthbert would not be unwilling to sell Bawdsey Manor, and so Wimperis and I returned to London with the feeling that we had found a probable answer to the problem of acquiring an isolated but not inaccessible property where experimental facilities could be provided without waiting for new buildings to be erected.

The purchase of this large property meant, for the first time, money in terms of five figures but, on the recommendation of the Tizard Committee, Sir Philip Cunliffe-Lister's Committee did not hesitate and Bawdsey Manor was bought by the Air Ministry.

So it came about that from the barren shingle and marshland of Orfordness the Islanders were transferred to the relatively exotic surroundings of Bawdsey Manor, with its spacious lawns, its peaches, its bougainvillaea and its sandy beach below the cliffs. In May 1936 Bawdsey Research

Station began its history, a history which terminated on the eve of 3 September 1939. It was a grand place for the work that had to be done and the only feature inappropriate to the new conceptions of defence which were born there was the motto above the door of the Manor, 'Plutôt mourir que changer'.

Before the birth of radar, the major gap in our defences was the inability to intercept, with sufficient frequency, mass formations of hostile bombers approaching our coasts in daylight. It was upon this problem that the work of Bawdsey Research Station was concentrated and the bulk of the Air Ministry staff worked upon it until the outbreak of war. It is therefore convenient at this stage to describe the evolution of the coastal radar chain from the installation of the first station at Bawdsey until, in 1939, a chain of stations from Ventnor to the Firth of Tay had so far passed out of the hands of scientists that even their visits to these stations were, with some justification, looked upon with suspicion. No dictum is so readily quoted to scientists by Service users of their products as 'The better is the enemy of the good'.

The scientists had shown the way, but others had now to play parts beyond the competence of the scientists. The Director of Signals at the Air Ministry (then Air Commodore Nutting) had to train men to maintain and operate the radar installations and the time was to come when these would be numbered in tens of thousands. The Director of Works and Buildings at the Air Ministry was faced with a great and indispensable task in civil engineering. Moreover, scientists are usually better at producing their results in 'lash-up' form than in evolving equipment which can be readily produced and easily maintained; in this respect the Bawdsey scientists were no exception. There was therefore a need for engineers, nearly all of whom were in industry, and it was to

PLATE II

BAWDSEY RESEARCH STATION, 1938

industry that the Air Ministry turned to supplement the work of the scientists.

By splendid co-operation between men of these different professions, the radar chain gradually took shape and men were trained in its operation. In February 1937 a training school for R.A.F. personnel was opened at Bawdsey under the command of Squadron-Leader R. G. Hart, who soon demonstrated that radar was not merely a toy for scientists but could be operated by Service personnel.

In May 1937 a radar-chain station, built within the confines of Bawdsey Research Station, was handed over entirely to R.A.F. personnel and so became the first prototype of stations which were, as an interim scheme, to cover the Thames Estuary. Dover followed in July and Canewdon (near Southend) became operational in August. The use of three radar stations brought new problems. An aircraft over the North Sea was commonly observed by two of the stations and often by all three of them. If each station told the same story of an aircraft position all was well but, alas, this rarely happened; small errors of calibration, minor aerial troubles and errors made by observers combined to give indications which often deserved the R.A.F. epithet of 'a dog's dinner'. It was clear that the several imperfect observations needed interpretation and so, in August 1937, Hart set up at Bawdsey an experimental 'filter room' with the object of sorting out the data received and establishing the most probable position of the observed aircraft.

The availability of three operational stations allowed radar, for the first time, to play an important part in an R.A.F. defence exercise, held in August 1937. From my London office, the radar results seemed nearer a failure than a success. Systematic and haphazard errors of the three stations made the task of assessing aircraft tracks extremely difficult; some aircraft approaching the coast were even recorded in the filter room as flying parallel with the coast. This apparent failure, caused by nothing more serious than hurried preparation and last minute modifications, needs to be recorded for two reasons: first, as an illustration that new developments often give disappointing results in the early stages, and secondly, as an illustration of the great faith of the Air Council in the ultimate success of radar. To go on involves more courage and more money while to stop means the loss of what might have been. A decision to rely on radar meant a reorientation of the existing plans for air defence, and in 1937 events across the water showed that time was pressing. To go on in spite of apparent failure, or not to go on, that was the question. Fortunately for this country, the Air Council and their advisers did not hesitate. Immediately after the August 1937 Exercises, orders were placed with industry for the equipment needed to instal twenty radar stations having a power and efficiency beyond the hopes of the Islanders of 1935. Magnificent pioneer work was done by Metropolitan Vickers on the transmitters and by Messrs Cossor on the receivers. These two firms initiated an effort which was to lead to a vast expansion of the radio industry.

The work involved in erecting, calibrating and manning these stations meant a tremendous effort on the part of several Air Ministry directorates, both Service and civilian. The Bawdsey research staff, in large part, stopped its research work and went out into the field to help, particularly with the difficult task of finding suitable sites and with the laborious and tricky business of calibrating the stations. Electricity and mud do not make good companions.

This was the position when I was privileged to take over the Superintendentship of the Bawdsey Research Station in May 1938 when Watson-Watt became the first Director of Communications Development at the Air Ministry. Let me say at this stage that I was not, and did not become, a radio expert as was my predecessor; but the change from a London office to close proximity to the scientists in the laboratories, to say nothing of the lawns and peaches and the bougainvillaea of Bawdsey, was so attractive that my protestations were not altogether sincere.

At this time, Bawdsey Research Station comprised about 150 men and women, including the cleaners. A handful of scientists were working on problems not concerned with the main coastal chain, problems to be described later. Most of the remainder were soon increasingly to be concerned with aiding the vast effort involved in installing the chain, but it was clear that research on the chain could not be altogether neglected. My chief worry, on taking charge at Bawdsey, was that the radar stations would be rendered useless by deliberate interference from hostile jamming stations. I therefore gave one of the scientific staff, E. C. Williams, the task of making his colleagues' lives a misery by deliberately jamming their equipment, a task in which he succeeded. With a modified diathermy transmitting set installed in a Sunderland aircraft he patrolled the east coast and caused consternation at the three existing radar chain stations and among his colleagues. It is typical of the growth of radar that awareness of a need is half-way to fulfilling it. When the dangers of jamming had been demonstrated, the ideas to combat them were not long in coming. Several solutions eventually played their part, the most important being one put forward by Professor T. R. Merton.

At least one other major problem needed solution. The radar scientists had determined the position of an aircraft by turning knobs and reading range and bearing on calibrated scales; height was found by reading another scale showing angle of elevation and then making a calculation. These readings had then to be corrected for errors known to be inherent in the chosen sites. All this took precious time and even then position was not obtained in a form suitable to Fighter Command, who used a grid system for plotting positions of aircraft. A solution of the difficulty was obtained, largely as a result of proposals by one of the Bawdsey staff, G. A. Roberts. An electrical converter was evolved, using automatic telephony technique, and known to the R.A.F. as the 'fruit machine', which enabled operators to press keys on their desks and so to transmit to the R.A.F. control data covering grid position, heights and estimated number of aircraft. Dowding, on seeing the electrical converter, said it would not be long before the scientists replaced the Com-mander-in-Chief of Fighter Command by a gadget!

Another success of this pre-war period was the first effec-tive contribution to the problem of distinguishing friend from foe, though it must be admitted that the problem re-mained partially unsolved throughout the war. In prin-ciple, the solution was for each coastal radar station to 'ask', in effect, whether an aircraft was friend or foe; if a friend, a special set in the aircraft caused the indications at the radar station to be distinctive. It was in the course of this work that Bawdsey Research Station suffered the first of many fatal casualties during experimental flying.

Work on the coastal chain gathered momentum and, with the Munich crisis of September 1938, five stations manned by R.A.F. personnel guarded the Thames Estuary. Then came a winter of mud and wind; mud for the scientists, engineers and fitters who installed the stations in the more desolate spots of Great Britain; wind for the men who worked hundreds of feet above the ground installing towers and aerial arrays. On Good Friday 1939 a chain of radar stations stretching from Ventnor to the Firth of Tay began a 24-hour watch which was scarcely to be interrupted until Germany was totally defeated.

The continuous manning of the whole coastal chain made a heavy demand on the resources of man-power available to the R.A.F. The use of women as radar observers had been proposed in 1937 and the time was ripe to put the proposal into effect. Three of the clerical staff of the Bawdsey Research Station quickly demonstrated, surely to the surprise of few, that women possess the conscientiousness, the patience and the sensitivity of touch necessary for the work. In October 1939 the first W.A.A.F. crew took over watch at Poling, near Arundel. To me, the publicity given to the use of women as radar observers has been hardly flattering to their sex. We have travelled far since Dr Johnson expressed surprise, not that a woman should preach well, but that she should preach at all. All honour to the women who shared with the men the often primitive and isolated conditions at the radar stations and who carried on with their tasks when the stations were attacked by the enemy; but in fact their task was no harder than many undertaken by women in factories and elsewhere.

We have come to know that to defend Great Britain only is not enough and so, in 1937, the thoughts of the R.A.F. authorities turned to the extension of radar cover to vulnerable points overseas. In September of that year I was sent by Air Marshal Sir Wilfred Freeman on a mission to the Middle East and to Malta to tell the Commanders-in-Chief of those areas of the coming of radar. Although working on the home chain up to the hilt of its pre-war resources, the Air Ministry soon began to erect radar stations at Malta, Aden and at other defended ports abroad.

This must be the end of my story of the first use of radar; of the creation of a chain of stations protecting our coasts by providing data on plan position, often at ranges of 100 miles and more, height and approximate numbers of the hostile aircraft approaching our coasts, thus enabling our fighter aircraft to intercept them. But of course it is not the end of the story of the evolution of the first radar chain. Not only Government scientists, but members of industrial firms and, not least, members of the R.A.F. continued to provide ideas for increasing the efficacy of the chain. The day was coming when radar research would move to Swanage where, carved in stone, are some appropriate and perhaps prophetic words by Pope:

> All served, all serving,
> Nothing stands alone.
> The chain holds on
> And where it ends unknown.

CHAPTER IV

WAVELENGTHS

ALTHOUGH radar played a dominant role in winning the Battle of Britain, this was but the beginning of its contribution to the defeat of Germany and of Japan. Other battles were to follow: the battle against the night bomber, the war at sea and the aerial battles of our bombers which carried the war into the heart of the territory of our enemies. The types of radar equipment which eventually played a decisive part in winning these battles had little resemblance to that used for the coastal chain; and just as the Wright brothers could hardly have been expected to visualize a Spitfire or a modern bomber, so, under the stress of war, types of radar were evolved which were beyond the visions of the Islanders. It is well that results in applied science are achieved in this way; to arrive at a perfect solution at the first attempt would be to rob scientists of that hopeful travel which constitutes, for them, the fascination of their profession.

The revolutionary advances made in radar technique during the war were largely associated with the attainment of greater and still greater transmitted powers on smaller and still smaller wavelengths and with the evolution of techniques for using the minute fractions of these powers which arrived at radar receiving stations. In order to appreciate much that follows, we had better deal with this business of wavelengths, even at the cost of a chronological break in the story.

It is easy to understand why radar was, from the beginning, impracticable without the radiation of large powers from transmitting aerials. We see aircraft in the sky, or flowers in a field, because the sun floodlights millions of square miles of the earth's surface, because an almost infinitesimal fraction of this light is scattered, or reradiated, by the aircraft or by the flowers and because a tiny fraction of this light is received by our eyes. If all that mattered in the world were that Tom Jones should see a few aircraft in the sky or a few flowers in a field, the sun would be a most inefficient source of energy, since most of its vast power would be wasted. If, at night, we wanted to see aircraft within several miles of us we might provide an enormous source of light on the ground which, by floodlighting the sky, would enable us to see them. But a far more practicable way of seeing an aircraft at night is to concentrate our light source into a beam and direct it on to the aircraft, i.e. to use a searchlight, and if we want to see several aircraft we can make the searchlight scan the skies and show us any aircraft within range. The first radar system, the coastal chain, used 'floodlighting', though means were adopted to project most of the radiated energy out to sea instead of inland. It is wonderful to contemplate that the power transmitted was sufficient to 'floodlight' tens of thousands of cubic miles of space, that a single aircraft in this vast space, flying at a distance sometimes as great as 200 miles from the transmitting station, could reradiate some of this energy, and not less wonderful to consider that an infinitesimal fraction of this scattered radiation could be sent back to the coastal radar station and be used to determine the position of the aircraft. To me, even the atomic bomb is less fantastic than this. It is important, however, to understand why, in spite of the success of floodlighting, the radar scientists sought to evolve a radio searchlight which they knew would open up fresh fields for the application of radar and why radar did not begin with the searchlight technique.

This brings us to some simple considerations regarding the choice of wavelengths for radar applications.

Long before 1935, when radar was born, large powers on wavelengths of tens, hundreds and thousands of metres were radiated by hundreds of broadcasting stations all over the world. All listeners were familiar with the process of tuning to 1,500 m. or to stations between 200 and 500 m., while many had sets capable of receiving wavelengths reckoned in tens of metres.

Before the birth of radar, the National Physical Laboratory scientists, working on the exploration of electrically charged layers far above the earth's surface, had used a wavelength of 50 m. The Daventry experiment described in Chapter 1 had been done with 50 m. To the Islanders this wavelength seemed about right. There was reason to suppose that the reradiation from an aircraft approaching a radar station would be a maximum if the wavelength used were double the span of the aircraft, and a length of 25 m., or roughly 80 ft., was not far from the average span of a bomber of that period. Experiments therefore started with 50 m., but it was soon found that reflections from the electrically charged layers, the old friends of the Islanders, caused confusion and a wavelength of 26 m. was tried. Troubles were less but still real and so the wavelength was reduced to 13 m. Later, when, to counter deliberate jamming, each coastal chain station used four different wavelengths, even smaller wavelengths were used but they were still several metres, and although splendid work was done by the Admiralty and by British Industry to increase the powers attainable on these wavelengths, the work was largely along known lines. Of useful powers on 1 m., there was hardly a sign of hope of early achievement.

It is one thing to develop special valves and circuits capable of generating tens and even hundreds of kilowatts of energy and quite another to design an aerial system which will transmit a useful proportion of these high powers. For transmitting purposes aerial arrays were evolved consisting of a number of carefully spaced individual aerial rods, each having a length of about one-half of the wavelength used; thus for a wavelength of 10 m., each aerial rod was 5 m. or about 15 ft. in length. These transmitting arrays were made more complicated by the reflecting arrays used to minimize the undesirable 'floodlighting' of inland territory. The receiving aerials were still more complicated because of the needs of direction and height-finding. It is not surprising therefore that aerial arrays for the wavelengths used in the coastal chain occupied thousands of cubic yards of space. Because each aerial rod needs to have a length of about half a wavelength it follows that the smaller the wavelength, the smaller are the aerial arrays used for transmission and reception.

The only serious shortcoming of the coastal chain, using wavelengths of several metres, was that it failed to detect at useful ranges the approach of low-flying aircraft. This was because the shape of the 'floodlit' zone of radiation left a gap in the region just above the surface of the sea. This phenomenon was not only a source of anxiety regarding defence against low-flying aircraft but apparently closed the door to hopes of locating hostile surface craft and submarines from our coasts or from our ships. In theory, the remedy was simple enough. The greater the ratio of the height of the aerial arrays to the wavelengths used, the easier it is to locate low-flying aircraft and surface vessels. But for the coastal chain, the height of the steel transmitting masts was already 350 ft. and that of the wooden receiving masts 240 ft. These masts had to be strong enough to support heavy aerial systems under conditions of wind and snow and, as has already been noted, the cost of a mast increases rapidly with its height. To increase mast height still further was not therefore a practical proposition, and the only alternative was to reduce the wavelength so that the ratio of aerial height (increased wherever possible by using a cliff site) to wavelength was large. But until 1938 useful powers were not available on wavelengths which afforded this solution of the problem of low cover.

A searchlight is able to scan the sky because its light source, reflector and casing can readily be physically swung in both horizontal and vertical planes to point in any direction. A radio searchlight must also be swung physically, though unsuccessful attempts have been made to produce a searchlight effect in other ways. We have seen that the longer the wavelength the larger the aerial system needs to be, and no engineer would lightly undertake the task of swinging mechanically the thousands of cubic yards of aerial array installed at the top of a tower hundreds of feet in height. If, however, useful powers could be produced on small wavelengths, then the smaller aerial systems could be mechanically swung with an ease which would depend upon the extent to which wavelength could be reduced.

Although the accuracy of the coastal chain, using 'floodlighting', was sufficient for the location of hostile bomber formations approaching by day, there was no doubt, from the earliest days of radar, that a radio searchlight using a narrow beam would give greater positional accuracy. This was a further incentive to the production of useful powers on wavelengths small enough to make radio searchlights practicable.

There was clearly hardly a limit to the usefulness of reducing wavelength, provided sufficient powers could be generated and received. If aerial systems could be made sufficiently small their installation in aircraft would be practicable, thus opening up vast new fields of application to war and to peace.

For these reasons there was an increasing urge during the late 1930's and throughout the war to produce useful powers on smaller and yet smaller wavelengths and to devise means for using them in receiver systems. The initial urge in this direction came primarily from Tizard, whose vision in these matters was a source of profound admiration to those who worked with him. Some of us were perhaps too dazzled by the outstanding success of the floodlighting system used in the coastal chain to see that it was but the primitive, if splendid, beginning of the technical history of radar.

The full story of the scientific work on valves, which led to a new era in radar, must be told by those who did the work. We at Bawdsey Research Station, and later elsewhere, were hardly more than greedy and impatient customers of their products. Having principally in mind the need for cover against low-flying aircraft, I remember standing on the cliffs of Bawdsey early in 1938 and saying: 'Oh for one kilowatt on a metre!' Before the year was out, more than a kilowatt was available on $1\frac{1}{2}$ m. and new applications of radar immediately became practicable. There is no doubt that much of the credit for the early successes obtained with shorter wavelengths belongs to the Admiralty (and particularly to C. S. Wright, their Director of Scientific Research), ably supported by Industry.

Successes with radar on $1\frac{1}{2}$ m. increased our hunger for useful powers on shorter and shorter wavelengths. The need for the utmost secrecy had hitherto restricted the number of scientific workers knowledgeable on radar and on its needs, but in the autumn of 1939 new teams containing some of the country's best physicists were set up at Birmingham (under M. L. E. Oliphant) and at the Clarendon Laboratory (under J. H. E. Griffiths, with the general guidance of Lindemann). Their task was the stupendous one of making radar practicable on a wavelength of 10 cm. In general, the Birmingham team concentrated upon generating useful powers on these tiny wavelengths and the Clarendon team on means for dealing with them in receiving systems. It was not long before the Birmingham team produced power of about 1 kW. on a wavelength of 10 cm.; this was an amazing achievement, and with the splendid aid of the Research Laboratories of the General Electric Company, a valve, known as a magnetron, suitable for production was available in July 1940.

It is usually idle to talk of the greatest victory, the greatest general or the greatest invention of a war; these matters are beyond assessment. I suppose, however, that few in a position to judge would hesitate to name the cavity magnetron as having had a more decisive effect on the outcome of the war than any other single scientific device evolved during the war. It was of far more importance than the atomic bomb, which had no effect at all on the outcome of the German war and contributed rather to the shortening of the Japanese war than to its result.

Work on generating higher and still higher powers went on throughout the war and the day was to come when not one, but hundreds of kilowatts, were to be generated on a wavelength of 10 cm. Meanwhile, equally brilliant work at the Clarendon Laboratory and by an Admiralty team enabled the reception problems on this wavelength to be solved to an extent which, during 1940, made applications of 10 cm. radar at least within the bounds of possibility.

It needs to be remembered that radar uses packets or pulses of energy, and during the drive to obtain higher powers it was essential not only to maintain at a small figure the length of time taken to emit a pulse but to make this time interval, or pulse width as it is called, even shorter. Using the analogy between radar and the echo of a shout from a cliff face, it will be appreciated that if one stands in front of

35   3-2

a cliff and gives a long shout, the echo will return to the shouter before his shout, or transmission, is complete. Every schoolboy knows that his shout must be sharp and short if he is to get a distinguishable echo and the nearer the cliff, the shorter the pulse of vocal transmission needs to be. For the coastal chain the 'shouts' or pulses of electromagnetic energy could be varied from 10 to 25 μsec., but for later applications they had to be, and were, as short as $\frac{1}{4}$ μsec. The concentration of tremendous powers into these short intervals was one of the miracles of radar.

Because in this book I am concentrating upon first-hand experiences, scant justice has been done to the work of the Admiralty, University and Industrial scientists who gave such splendid tools to those whose task it was to apply radar to the needs of war. Let me record, however, that no equal number of scientists did more than these to bring about the defeat of our enemies.

CHAPTER V

MORE OF BAWDSEY

As hope of peace in our time gave way to the inevitability of war, Bawdsey Research Station grew not only in knowledge but in strength. An increasing number of young men in flannel trousers were to be seen travelling by foot, cycle, bus or car of ancient vintage, along the road from Felixstowe to Felixstowe Ferry and then packing themselves into a little ferry boat manned by one of the many Suffolk Brinkleys. Charlie Brinkley had a steel hook in place of one arm and to this day the R.A.F. stores vocabulary designates a piece of radio test equipment as a 'Brinkley Earthing Stick'. Visitors to Felixstowe were puzzled by strange happenings across the River Deben; great towers sprouting from the lovely grounds of Bawdsey Manor caused one visitor to say to another: 'If I owned that house I would have an indoor aerial.'

In spite of concentration upon the coastal chain, a few fortunate scientists were able to work towards, if not indoor aerials, at any rate smaller radar systems which could take advantage of the useful powers on smaller wavelengths which now began to be available.

Reference has been made to the inability of the coastal chain to see low-flying aircraft and as Fighter Command became more cheerful about intercepting medium- and high-flying aircraft by the use of radar, so that body became more concerned about the danger of wave-hopping aircraft slipping through our radar cover. The problem was solved not only because smaller wavelengths became available but also because of some splendid work by a team of War Office scientists at Bawdsey. The full story of the work of this team is best told by one of their number but it is proper that full credit should be given for its contribution to the solution of a Royal Air Force problem. With the success of the Orfordness experiments, the Army Council had become immediately alive to the possibilities of radar, and at the end of 1936 the first War Office scientists were attached to Bawdsey to work on radar for anti-aircraft gunnery control. Towards the end of 1938 an augmented team of War Office scientists attacked the problem of the location of ships from the shore. By the summer of 1939, they had not only succeeded in measuring ranges of ships with an accuracy of about 20 yards but had devised a new and elegant method of measuring the bearing of a ship to within a few minutes of arc. Because the need for cover against low-flying aircraft was more important than ship-spotting, the reward of these scientists was to have their set taken from them. This set, when modified for its new purpose, was the forerunner of an additional chain of radar stations which eventually surrounded our coasts; it was known as the C.H.L. (C for Chain, H for Home and L for Low flying). By using a wavelength of $1\frac{1}{2}$ m., the aerial systems were small enough to be rotated on turntables and so form part of a radar searchlight.

In June 1939 the location of a low-flying aircraft approaching Bawdsey was demonstrated to Winston Churchill and this was the only occasion on which, throughout years of demonstrations to many of the greatest in the land, there was a mild attempt at cheating in order to produce a spectacular effect. After Winston Churchill had seen on a radar screen the approach of an aircraft at the low-flying height of 200 ft., he was led out to watch the passage of the aircraft over the station; the pilot had been asked to drop height still farther, just before the coast was crossed, in an attempt to remove the great man's hat with the slipstream.

The pilot was however rightly cautious and the hat remained on its impressive perch.

Early in the history of radar development, Watson-Watt had forecast that radar sets would one day be installed in aircraft. This was indeed vision of the boldest kind. To put the conception in its correct perspective, it need only be said that, even at the end of the war, Germany had failed to do more than use an elementary form of radar set in aircraft. The problem was to make radar sets small, light, easy to operate and yet serve their purpose. A constant and understandable struggle goes on between the aircraft designer and those who, in his view, seek to ruin his work by the installation of gadgets. The aircraft designer asks only that aircraft shall fly fast, far and high and, in effect, he says to the radar man: 'I put my brains into producing high-performance aircraft and, with your additional loads and your protruding aerials, you make them into Christmas trees.' The radar man replies: 'What is the use of your aircraft if it does not do its job, which it certainly will not do without radar?' Somehow a balance must be held and tempers kept. During the war it often seemed to the radar man that, in Germany, the aircraft designer always won the argument.

The earliest work on aircraft radar was directed towards the location of a night bomber by a radar-fitted night fighter. The problem was entirely different from that of the interception of hostile formations by day; for the latter an accuracy of location of a mile or two sufficed, while for the former the night-fighter pilot needed to be given 'eyes' which would 'see' beyond his normal vision of a few hundred feet. The voices which most loudly urged a solution of the night problem were those of Tizard and Dowding, while the scientist chiefly responsible for meeting the call was E. G. Bowen, a member of the Bawdsey Research Station. A night-fighter pilot needs to know the direction in which to fly in order to engage a hostile bomber and he needs to have a continuous record of the distance between himself and the enemy; this latter enables him to gauge his speed of approach, to settle down on the tail of a hostile bomber and to know when to open fire. The airborne radar group, as it was called, started work at Bawdsey in the autumn of 1936. Crude equipment was flying in an Anson aircraft by the summer of 1937 but until 1939 only range measurements were obtained; clearly it was of little use for a night-fighter pilot to know that an enemy aircraft was a mile away if he had no means of intercepting it.

Although the airborne radar group had to wait more than two years before reaching the first practical solution of the problem of night-fighter location of a hostile bomber (the primary reason for setting up the group), its early work is an outstanding example of how organizations and new projects are born in the world of applied science. Before describing the apparently incidental fruits of their labours, it is well to record the outstanding achievement of this group in reaching a first solution of its main task, i.e. to enable a fighter pilot to 'see' at night and to intercept his prey. During 1939 the airborne radar group evolved an aerial system with switching devices which enabled a night-fighter pilot to determine whether an aircraft flying somewhere in front of him was above or below and to the left or to the right. With a knowledge of range, this information enabled a night-fighter pilot to 'home' on to an enemy bomber and to engage it from astern. During the war, radar in aircraft was to prove perhaps an even more important factor in the Allied victory than was the use of ground radar installations; all honour then to this small British team which, in the late 1930's, laid the foundations of aircraft radar.

Let us now see how a new organization and a new project arose from the work of the airborne radar group.

Before the war, the Royal Air Force could ill afford to allocate aircraft for experimental work, and scientists' engaged in different fields were often forced to share an aircraft, to the confusion of all concerned. The first experiments in aircraft radar were no exception to this custom, but it soon became clear that the work of the airborne radar group at Bawdsey deserved special consideration. Accordingly, in 1938, a flight of aircraft located at Martlesham Aerodrome was allocated solely for radar experiments. None could then know that a giant had been born. As the Bawdsey Research Station moved from place to place and was given one name after another, the number of aircraft provided and maintained by the Royal Air Force, solely for the use of the radar scientists, grew apace. Only during the awful summer of 1940 was there a danger that their experimental aircraft would be taken from them and thrown into the Battle of Britain. Had this been done, the adverse effect on the war would have been incalculable. By 1940 our Research Establishment had its own small aerodrome and aircraft which came nominally under my control, although of course all matters affecting the control of R.A.F. personnel and the handling of aircraft came under an R.A.F. officer. The appetites of the scientists for aircraft grew with their successes and more and more aircraft of the latest types were needed for their work. During the last years of the war, Defford, one of the largest aerodromes in the country, was devoted solely to serving the needs of the radar scientists. The management of this aerodrome, operating nearly a hundred aircraft of all sorts and sizes, was a big job in itself and the R.A.F. took over sole control, putting the aerodrome under the command of a Group-Captain. All this had grown from the R.A.F. provision in 1938 of a small flight at Martlesham to serve the needs of the radar scientists. As my story continues, the outstanding achievements of aircraft radar will become apparent. Let it be said that the work of the scientists would have been of no avail without the tireless efforts of the R.A.F. officers and men who flew and maintained aircraft for civilian scientists. Now that the deeds of radar have been publicly disclosed, it is to be hoped that the many R.A.F. personnel who counted as lost all the time not spent in contact with the enemy, will understand that modern war involves more than the heat of battle.

The earliest and, in my view, most far-reaching practical result achieved by the handful of scientists who set out in 1936 to discover how to apply radar to the needs of night fighting was the location of ships from aircraft. The time was to come when, by night or by day, in clear weather or foul, no surfaced submarine was safe from radar observations even at distances of 15 miles, and often more from a patrolling aircraft. Stimulated by a question from Air Marshal Joubert, the A.O.C.-in-C. of Coastal Command, the Bawdsey airborne radar group installed an aircraft with the first A.S.V. (Air to Surface Vessel) equipment, and two years before the outbreak of war, to the very day, strong responses were obtained from H.M.S. *Rodney* and H.M.S. *Courageous* at a range of five miles. Here again we see the familiar pattern of my story: stimulation from a prospective user, the birth of a project and the first triumph with crude equipment having a radar performance which later was to seem insignificant. From this beginning it was not long before specially fitted aerials enabled an aircraft to 'home' on to a surface vessel; this, had they known, was the writing on the wall for the German Submarine Service.

The progress described in this chapter was the work of those few of the Bawdsey staff who could be spared from work on the coastal chain and it brings to an end my story of the pre-war days. At the outbreak of the war, the scientific strength of the Bawdsey Research Station was about one hundred, and that of the airborne radar group had grown to about a dozen. It is not an easy matter to assess the work of these pioneers in relation to that done by the hundreds of scientists recruited for radar during the war. It is a recognition rather than a disparagement of their work to say that, with three or four exceptions, the Bawdsey scientists were of average ability and that the percentage of genius was greatly increased by recruitment from the Universities and from Industry during the war. The pioneers achieved their unforgettable results by working at war intensity with an enthusiasm born of a knowledge of the greatness of their task.

CHAPTER VI

WAR

BECAUSE, with the outbreak of war, the Bawdsey research staff was to be scattered over three countries and to reach the lowest ebb of its fortunes, it is perhaps well to review what had by then been achieved and what had not. In particular, it is important to examine the extent to which radar was ready for war and to see why the Bawdsey staff, working splendidly together as a team, was scattered over the length and breadth of Great Britain.

In later years, the applications of radar to the tasks of the R.A.F. became well defined; there was the defence against air attack by day, defence against night bombers, the sea war (specially the problem of the submarine) and the provision of means enabling our bombing aircraft to find and to hit their targets. So let us take stock of how far radar had provided practical solutions of these very different tasks by that fateful day, 3 September 1939.

At the outbreak of war, the coastal radar chain was giving cover against hostile air attack by day, from Aberdeen to Southampton. Except on low-flying aircraft, ranges of 60 and 70 miles were everyday occurrences and 100 miles was often exceeded. The early Bawdsey experiments on filtering had borne fruit, and already there was at the Stanmore Headquarters of Fighter Command a room which absorbed and filtered masses of data regarding movements of aircraft in the areas off our eastern and southern coasts. From some coastal stations, though not from all, the height of approaching aircraft could be found with sufficient accuracy and assessment of numbers could be made with an accuracy sufficient to enable Fighter Command to dispose its precious

44

fighters to the best advantage. Only identification of friend from foe was not yet available to the R.A.F. To provide radar data is one thing and to use it quite another. By the outbreak of war the R.A.F. had revolutionized its plans for defence against hostile formations of aircraft and had evolved a scheme based on radar. The seeds of this revolution had been sown by Tizard who, even before radar data were available, proposed that controlled interception experiments should be conducted on the assumption that radar information was reaching the fighter pilot. The experiments were made at Biggin Hill and an important angle used in the process of mock interception was known as the 'Tizzy' angle.

Although it was not until the Battle of Britain that the coastal chain performed its indispensable task against the enemy, it was ready on the outbreak of war. From being beyond the realms of possibility in January 1935, the radar chain was ready in September 1939; ready to give data on the movements of mass formations of hostile aircraft and so enable our meagre fighter strength to be used to the full.

At the outbreak of war, radar had provided no working system of defence against night attack and no other was available. A number of $1\frac{1}{2}$ m. experimental A.I. (Air Interception) equipments had been flown which enabled a night-fighter pilot to home on to a bomber, provided that the bomber was not more than two miles distant and not at a distance greater than the height of the fighter above the ground; this latter restriction was a grave disadvantage against bombers flying at low and medium heights. One of the great problems engaging the airborne radar group was to make the radar pulse so narrow that a fighter pilot could home on to a bomber until visual contact was made. For this purpose, on the analogy of the shout against the cliff, the pulse needed to be less than 3 μsec. for the minimum

45

distance of 400 yards attained by the outbreak of war; even so, the A.O.C.-in-C. of Fighter Command was strong in his demand for a much shorter minimum distance of operation. All this work was, however, experimental. Because, before 3 September 1939, only a handful of staff had been engaged on the night-defence problem, airborne radar equipment had not reached the production stage, few R.A.F. personnel had been trained to use it and no satisfactory system of night defence had been evolved.

Few of the early successes at Bawdsey were to have such far-reaching consequences as the location in September 1937 of two battleships by means of radar installed in an aircraft; yet in the pre-war years little progress was made and in September 1939 no A.S.V. (the aircraft set for surface-ship location) was available to the R.A.F.

Viewed with the knowledge that a crucial war was nearly upon us, a war nowhere more dangerous to our cause than at sea, it may seem surprising that the splendid experimental success of 1937 was not followed up more rapidly. To those of us however who, in those pre-war days, dealt with science for defence purposes there is nothing surprising about the rate of progress achieved. The few scientific staff faced with breaking new ground in fitting aircraft with radar for night defence was the same staff that had the task of developing radar for the sea war. It is my purpose to tell of the pre-war days as they really were; let me say therefore that we simply failed to recruit an adequate scientific staff for the work to be done. Let me say also that this was not because the Air Ministry refused sanction for an increased staff or because the Treasury refused to supply the money, but largely because few first-class scientists could be attracted to work on defence problems. Whenever, by the promise of fascinating but vaguely defined work or by the display to a potential recruit of the beauties of Bawdsey

Manor, a scientist could be persuaded to join the Bawdsey team, Headquarters' authority was never withheld. The fact remains, however, that the scientific man-power was not available to provide the R.A.F. with A.S.V. by the outbreak of war.

The time was to come when radar would enable Bomber Command to cripple Germany but of this, in September 1939, there was no sign. It is true that the already overwhelmed airborne radar group at Bawdsey had installed equipment in an aircraft which, by providing rough measurements of height above the ground, gave a faint hope of navigating aircraft by comparing the height readings with contour maps; moreover, the passage of an aircraft over a coast, at night or through cloud, was usually observable with this equipment. Time was to show that the decision not to follow up this line of development was correct. It is, in fact, fair to say that, at the outbreak of war, radar had provided nothing for Bomber Command, nor was it universally appreciated that Bomber Command was in need of a revolutionary advance if it was to find and hit its targets. I remember, in 1939, giving my opinion that half the Bawdsey staff should be engaged on aids to Bomber Command; I must confess, however, that this was no more than a dim realization of a need to come and not a conviction that Bomber Command could be aided along lines then known.

This summary of progress made at Bawdsey deals only with radar applications to the Royal Air Force. The War Office team at Bawdsey was meanwhile opening new fields for the application of radar, particularly for the blind fire of A.A. guns; their story however needs to be told by one of them.

Until the year 1939 the development of radar was almost wholly the work of Government scientists, ably supported by Industry. Even within Government circles few scientists outside Bawdsey were aware of the progress being made, while fewer still of our leading scientists in the Universities were aware of the Bawdsey work. Notable exceptions were the members of the Tizard Committee and, later, Lord Rutherford. In 1939 it became clear that the scientific manpower of the country would soon need to be harnessed for the miserable business of war. The Royal Society therefore undertook the vital task of classifying the extent and nature of the scientific effort that could be made available in war. As a result of this onerous task, a number of eminent and not so eminent scientists from the Universities, including professors, lecturers and research workers, were shown round the Government Research Establishments, including Bawdsey. One, W. B. Lewis, who in 1945 was to become my successor as Chief Superintendent, joined the Bawdsey team several months before the war. Others were to join us when the war had begun, but already they had spent much of their University vacations on preparing themselves for the tasks ahead, tasks then beyond their comprehension.

This is perhaps the moment to pay tribute to the contribution made to radar by these University scientific workers who surely had never imagined themselves as civil servants, however temporary. A very few were hopelessly unfitted for work on applied science and other spheres of effort had to be found for them. Nearly all found difficulty in adapting themselves to the atmosphere of Government research. Few understood that there was a reasonable method of obtaining a screwdriver, for which the taxpayer paid, other than by walking out and buying it. The usual methods of maintaining some kind of discipline, if the word is applicable at all in research work, were not practicable. Few of these men cared about promotion or recognition and the sole object of most was to get the war over and to return to fundamental scientific work in their Universities.

It is useless to deny that some of the best of these University men caused me sleepless nights but, as years went on, the best traditions of Government science and the best traditions of University research were welded together and a team was formed of which I cannot even now think without emotion. During their work for the R.A.F. the University scientists came gradually to understand that a laboratory effect was not enough; that it was but the beginning of the long road to the production of a device usable by the R.A.F. They came to understand, too, that some law and order in security and other matters is not merely 'red tape'. On the other hand, the University scientists brought to the Government service a freshness of outlook, unhampered by conceptions of loyalty and discipline appropriate to the fighting Services; and they brought genius.

On balance, I am certain of this; without these specially recruited University men, the few scientists of equal calibre, recruited under pre-war Civil Service conditions, would not have come within sight of achieving radar as it is known to-day.

When, in 1936, Bawdsey Manor was chosen as the site for radar research, opposition was not lacking. Many felt that its high towers on the coast of the North Sea would make it a conspicuous and easy target for our likely enemy. On the other hand, there were those, among whom I number myself, who felt that the need for speed was so great that the most suitable site in the British Isles should be chosen, irrespective of its security. As a compromise it was agreed that radar research should be done at Bawdsey but that the scientific personnel should be immediately evacuated in the event of war.

Early in 1939 there was no longer much doubt that the small team carefully and with difficulty built up since 1935 was soon to be scattered, though we did not then know that it would be dispersed over three countries. Arrangements had been made, we then thought, for the majority of the scientific staff to move into quarters at Dundee should war begin, and for the airborne radar group to go to the aerodrome of Perth some 20 miles from Dundee. A few of the staff who had shown administrative as well as scientific abilities were earmarked for duty under Watson-Watt at Headquarters, for without an adequate Headquarters' backing, the work of a research Establishment is gravely handicapped. Two other groups were to be detached from the parent body at Dundee; one was to go to Leighton Buzzard and the other to the Headquarters of Fighter Command at Stanmore. In pursuance of my task of describing how organizations, as well as scientific projects, are born, the reasons for the Leighton Buzzard and Stanmore detachments need separate consideration. From small beginnings these detachments were to grow to world-wide organizations.

Before the war, and indeed until the spring of 1940, the small team of research workers responsible for radar projects for the R.A.F. had also the responsibility of supervising the installation and maintenance of the whole coastal chain. This was not research work but it had to be done. The R.A.F. was training maintenance crews as rapidly as possible, but expert knowledge was still largely in the possession of civilian scientists who were sent far afield to supervise an installation or a calibration or to investigate a breakdown. With a knowledge of later events, the work of these few men seems beyond understanding and beyond praise.

It was clear that, if the Bawdsey research workers moved to Dundee, some more central location would have to be chosen for the small team engaged on nursing the coastal chain, and a search was made for suitable quarters. For me, the story of radar will always be associated with the search for places where the research staff could work and live. In the summer of 1939 Dewhurst, the head of the team, found a house of moderate size at Leighton Buzzard and arrangements were made to ensure that, in the event of war, the work of his team could be continued from there with the least possible interruption. This was the origin of a vast R.A.F. organization, involving tens of thousands of officers and men; the origin in February 1940 of 60 Group which, at the end of the war, was under the command of an Air Vice-Marshal.

So much publicity has been given to operational research and to its influence on the successful outcome of the war, that some account of its origin and original objectives may be thought to fit into the pattern of my story.

There is, of course, nothing new about research on the results of warlike operations. For thousands of years, admirals and generals have pored over the details of their battles and have sought to analyse the causes of victory or defeat. No doubt in prehistoric times there were objective discussions on whether an enemy would be the more discomfited by a rapid barrage of small stones or by the less speedy process of throwing big ones.

My definition of operational research, as conducted in the war, is the use of civilian scientists át the Headquarters of the Service chiefs; i.e. at Command Headquarters, or, less commonly, at the three Service Ministries. During the war the great majority of operational research workers were so employed.

Close understanding between those who use weapons of war and the defence scientists had been a pet theme of mine since the early 1920's. While serving under Wimperis, I had the task of examining ideas received from sources outside the Air Ministry, and I was struck with the rarity with which a suggestion of any value was put forward by anyone not knowledgeable on Service needs. Moreover, I could not (and do not now) understand why great efforts were made to instruct serving officers in scientific matters while no efforts were made to instruct scientists in the theory of war. I recall proposing, in the 1920's, that a number of scientists should be sent annually to the Staff Colleges, but the time was not ripe.

In 1939, I gave much thought to how a union of Service user and scientist could be effected during the coming war. In the summer of that year Squadron-Leader Hart, who had been a splendid friend to the scientists during his stay at Bawdsey, was stationed at Fighter Command Headquarters and I proposed to him that, at the outbreak of war, a few of the Bawdsey scientists should be attached to him for work at the very centre of air defence operations. By this arrangement I hoped both to give and to get. I hoped to give Fighter Command the services of men who had an intimate knowledge of the performance of the radar chain and who had, as scientists, been trained to use their analytical faculties; and I hoped to get from my detached members of staff the true facts concerning the operations against the enemy, and so enable the Bawdsey staff to be permeated with an intimate knowledge of the needs of Fighter Command.

This informal undertaking with Hart worked splendidly; a team under Harold Larnder, who gave greatly of himself during the war, was earmarked for Fighter Command on the outbreak of war. It is not my purpose to give the history of operational research but only to use it as an example of how great organizations are born and of how, like radar itself, a scheme can blossom far beyond the scope and purpose of its original conception. Suffice it here to say that the small team sent to Fighter Command became, more formally, the Stanmore Research Section, working to the day-to-day instructions of Fighter Command but owing allegiance to its parent body at Dundee. After a year or so of war it was obvious that operational research was going to spread and that it was illogical for it to be controlled from one Establishment working in one field of effort. Other arrangements were therefore rightly made for its future.

The first day of September 1939 found Bawdsey Research Station with packing cases waiting alongside the laboratories. All arrangements had been made for the journey north and only word from Headquarters was awaited. In our conceit, it was felt probable that the enemy would bomb the Manor in the first hours of the war and perhaps even before war was declared; but Bawdsey Manor still stands.

It was on this day that the Germans crossed the Polish frontier, and packing began. The miserable business of waiting for what seemed certain was over and my chief feeling was one of relief that the task of doing something to end an intolerable dependence on Hitler's speeches could at last begin.

This was the end of Bawdsey Research Station. The War Office team went to Christchurch to found a new Establishment; Dewhurst's team went to Leighton Buzzard to found 60 Group; Larnder's team left for Stanmore to found operational research; several left to serve Watson-Watt at Headquarters; two scientists, lent from another Government department, returned to their homes to collect their belongings for the journey north and I never saw them again. The rest packed themselves into lorries and cars and went north towards Dundee.

At eleven o'clock on 3 September 1939, in a little cottage in Northumberland, I heard Neville Chamberlain announce that we were at war.

CHAPTER VII

DUNDEE

W E could hardly continue to be called Bawdsey
Research Station when working in the middle of
Dundee. We might, of course, have become known
as the Dundee Research Station, but perhaps some prophetic sense told Headquarters that Dundee was to be but
an incident and that our travels were only beginning; at
any rate the new title chosen for us was the Air Ministry
Research Establishment (A.M.R.E.) which effectively
disguised our concern with radar. After writing of the
pioneer work at Orfordness and of the great days of
Bawdsey, I confess I find it difficult to write seriously of
our stay in Dundee. We started badly enough. On my
arrival at the buildings we understood we were to occupy,
I was confronted with the news that there was no accommodation for us and that our equipment was being dumped
in the open. My representations to those responsible for
the buildings, who incidentally were guiltless in the matter,
produced a slight but totally inadequate concession. I
was told (and I wish my pen could produce the Scottish
flavour) that if we could not be welcomed we would be
tolerated and, in this spirit, two rooms were offered us.
Thus began our war history. From the spacious buildings
and grounds of Bawdsey Manor we were to be reduced to
two rooms, though I never discovered whether we were
entitled to the parking space occupied by our packing cases.
Fortunately, a partial solution was found within a day.
Hearing of our plight, Professor McLelland, the Principal
of the Dundee Training College, cleared a floor and a half
of his spacious and attractive building and, until we left

Dundee, continued to give all assistance in his power. Yet although at this time we reached our lowest ebb, some good things happened in Dundee. Men joined us there who, in time, were to be members of the inner circle of the grand team that eventually emerged: J. A. Ratcliffe, who later controlled one-third of the Establishment; H. B. Skinner and A. G. Ward who, although not born to be civil servants, were the keystone of much of the fundamental work which widened the scope of radar, and D. M. Robinson, who later was to play a leading part in the radar collaboration between this country and the U.S.A. A Fighter Command demand that the airborne radar set for intercepting night bombers should have a minimum range of only 100 ft., led to the beginning of a long and fruitful collaboration with the Electrical and Musical Industries research team, a collaboration that, three years later, was to cost leading members of the team their lives. Another event of this gloomy period was a collaboration with the War Office team at Christchurch which led to the availability of C.H.L. stations. By mid-1940, these stations provided low cover from South Wales to Scotland and so shared with the coastal chain the radar honours of the Battle of Britain. By the courtesy of the R.A.F., some useful work was also done at a coastal chain station several miles from Dundee.

But, with these exceptions, it is difficult to find good in the Dundee era of what was now A.M.R.E. If however we were seemingly bankrupt it is not to be supposed that grand work was not done elsewhere. Dewhurst's team at Leighton Buzzard was showing the need for a large organization for maintaining the coastal radar stations, the need for a 60 Group soon to be formed. Larnder's team at Fighter Command was fulfilling all my hopes of collaboration between Service user and civilian scientist and was paving the way for the vast expansion of operational research which was to come in later years. Of one radar effort of the period it is not my business to speak, but few knowledgeable on the history of radar will forget the work of J. D. Cockcroft and his team of newly recruited University workers, who used the splendid fruits of the British Radio Industry to instal coast defence sets for use against submarines and aircraft.

While others were making important contributions to radar history, it was clear, early in 1940, that our immediate task was to pack once more and move elsewhere. Already the airborne radar Group at Perth, under Bowen, had found the Scottish winter and other factors unsuitable for intensive research involving aircraft, and in November 1939 the Group moved to St Athan in South Wales. Thus it came about that A.M.R.E. at Dundee was, in theory, controlling the work of teams in South Wales, at Leighton Buzzard and at Stanmore. The reasons for the unsuitability of Dundee were not in doubt; the middle of a great city, with its electrical disturbances and its lack of open spaces, was about the last place to choose for radar research and all concerned with selecting or not opposing the Dundee site, including myself, had learned a lesson not to be forgotten.

Now came a search for a suitable site and our spirits rose in the process. We needed a large and fairly flat isolated area; we needed a cliff site, proximity to electric power, proximity to an aerodrome and to a town where the staff could live. We needed also to be reasonably near London yet as far as possible from enemy activity. Finally, a site was found which stretched from the charming village of Worth Matravers in Dorsetshire to the lovely cliffs of St Alban's Head, with Swanage as the nearest town. The greatest weakness of the site was that the aerodrome chosen for our work was at Christchurch, 20 miles distant. We were not then to know that our remoteness from enemy activity was to be short-lived, though, in the event, we suffered little and gained much from his proximity, at least until the day, two years later, when we were to pack yet again.

In those early days of the Establishment's history it was not a difficult task to take up our equipment and move elsewhere since our maximum strength at Dundee was only 400. The task of the Works department of the Air Ministry was, however, more onerous. Huts had to be built for us at Worth Matravers, roads had to be made, electric power had to be provided and, because we had not then emerged from the era of metre wavelengths, 350 ft. steel and 240 ft. wooden towers had to be built for experiments with the type of radar equipment used for the coastal chain. It is fashionable to curse 'Works and Bricks' but it was my experience through 10 years of contact with radar that the Air Ministry Department of Works rendered an inestimable service to the scientists. I was not therefore surprised that we were soon able to leave Dundee for Worth Matravers.

No family of city dwellers has packed for its seaside holiday with more zest than we brought to the task of moving from Dundee, and on 5 May 1940 we moved southward in convoy.

It is perhaps worth while noting why the Dundee era was a failure. First, the team built up by Watson-Watt, and extended during my period of Superintendentship at Bawdsey, had been scattered, and although some brilliant men had joined us after the outbreak of war, the task of mixing them with what was left of the pre-war team was not easy. Secondly, the facilities for our work were inadequate and there was little chance of improving morale by achieving successes. To make matters worse I had risked offending my old colleagues by appointing Lewis as my deputy, though he had been with us but a few months. Living conditions in Dundee did nothing to raise our spirits and what was surely the blackest black-out in Great Britain was not made more bearable by the barricades of sandbags on the pavements.

Dundee is an example of a conviction I have regarding the conduct of an applied research Establishment. If it is in the doldrums, do something big; disband it, move it elsewhere or bring in fresh blood at the top. We moved elsewhere.

CHAPTER VIII

WORTH MATRAVERS

IN the years that were to come the most common tribute paid to the Establishment was that it worked as a team which believed in its task. Although in those early days of Worth Matravers a team did not exist, the constituent material from which the team emerged was being collected in one geographical spot. The Dundee contingent was followed within a day by the arrival from South Wales of the airborne radar group of the Bawdsey days, their ranks having been increased by men such as A. C. B. Lovell and A. Hodgkin, who were to show themselves to be of great stature. Dewhurst's team at Leighton Buzzard was disbanded on the formation, under the inspiring leadership of Air Commodore A. L. Gregory, of the R.A.F. 60 Group they had founded; some put on uniform and in time became rather surprised squadron-leaders and wing-commanders while others swelled the ranks of Worth Matravers. An event which was to have a profound influence on the Establishment was the arrival of P. I. Dee, looking something like his alleged ancestor, the Wizard of Upton. Yet another event of great significance for the future was the arrival of a large contingent from the Radio Department of the Royal Aircraft Establishment, South Farnborough. Some of them were Government Servants of long standing, while others had been recruited from Industry and from the Universities. Among them were four men, R. Cockburn, C. Holt Smith, D. Fry and A. H. Reeves who, having little in common, were to make splendid contributions in their different ways.

Here then was excellent material for the future Establishment; but it was not a team. Some were civil servants

59

accustomed to work in a well-defined organization; others, chiefly from the Universities, either did not know what organization meant or did not believe in it. Some wanted to rush into new radar applications for the R.A.F. while others urged that years of fundamental work were needed before the application stages could be reached. Some, conscious of their status in previous fields of work, wanted to control a large staff while others, including two or three of the most able, wanted a small corner in which to work, with freedom from the administrative cares associated with running a staff. Many of the most able men were strangers to one another and mutual respect was yet to be born. Surely the witches' cauldron contained no more indigestible a mixture than did the heterogeneous staff of A.M.R.E. in the early summer of 1940. The task of distributing the staff among different war objectives would have been easier had the progress of the war shown more clearly where radar effort was needed. Norway had been lost but there were no important repercussions on the A.M.R.E. programme; perhaps because there were no lessons to be learnt in the radar field, or because an intimate association of operational user and laboratory scientist was yet to come. Holland, Belgium and then France were lost but still there were few calls on A.M.R.E. specifically related to these events. Then came the Battle of Britain which was to be the great test of the coastal radar chain, on which most of the efforts of the radar scientists since 1935 had been spent. Here, in the sky, were the long-awaited formations of hostile aircraft approaching our coasts; there, on the radar screens around our eastern and southern coasts, were the long-visualized indications which enabled our fighter aircraft to take an increasing toll of the enemy. Still there were no great demands on A.M.R.E. of the kind that came in later years. Some assistance was of course given to the R.A.F. in their

great task, particularly in regard to countering radio interference, but it was soon clear that the planning of the
Directorate of Signals, Air Ministry, and of Fighter Command for the operation of the coastal radar chain had been
effective. I used often, in the pre-war days, to say that the
defence scientist was at war in time of peace and thus it was
that the radar scientists had evolved in time of peace a
defence weapon which was to preserve this country in the
summer of 1940. The Battle of Britain was the first of several
decisive battles of the war which largely depended upon
radar for victory.

Although no current war operations made great demands
on A.M.R.E. few doubted, in the summer of 1940, that
Fighter Command would soon have to face a new battle,
the battle against the night bomber. With the coming of
the longer nights it was certain that, if Britain survived the
day bombing, she would be faced with bombing by night.
Let it be said plainly that, at that time, no effective answer
had been found to the night bomber. It is part of my story
to tell how the radar scientists found an answer, and the
speed with which their proposals were made effective is a
tribute not only to the scientists but to the R.A.F. Signals
and Fighter Command organizations which took the revolutionary devices of the scientists and made them the everyday
tools of Service personnel.

We had better be clear about the magnitude of the problem of defence against air attack by night, a problem
totally different from that presented by formations of aircraft attacking by day. During daylight, radar inaccuracies
of a mile or two, height errors of two or three thousand feet,
or delays of a minute or two in passing information through
a filter room and through a Sector H.Q. to the day-fighter
squadrons, were not serious; provided that the fighter aircraft could be directed with sufficient accuracy for them to

see their bomber targets, superior speed did the rest. How different was the night problem! The German Air Force had not learnt, and never did learn, how to use highly concentrated forces of night bombers of the kind used later by Bomber Command and so German night bombers were sent over singly, at intervals of a few minutes, making crossings of the coast at scattered points. It was, in fact, calculated that, in an average night raid during the winter of 1940–41, there was one German bomber to every 900 cubic miles of space. In brilliant moonlight an important degree of success could occasionally be achieved without reliance upon radar, but on average nights it was clear that only some new conception of air defence could enable a night fighter to find its target in a vast volume of darkness. The pre-war work at Bawdsey on the use of an aircraft radar set to enable a fighter aircraft to home on to the tail of a bomber has been described but, apart from the fact that in the summer of 1940 few of these sets were available, it was clear that A.I. could not alone provide the needed solution of night defence.

The maximum range of the A.I. set was not more than two miles and, somehow or other, means had to be found for guiding the night fighter to such a position with respect to the enemy that its A.I. set could be effectively used. There are two separate parts to the story of how the radar scientists solved the problem of night defence against air attack and, in giving them individual attention, we shall see how teams began to emerge from the heterogeneous collection of scientists who arrived at Worth Matravers in the early summer of 1940. We shall also see, once again, how a revolutionary advance in radar technique was born of a user need. The Battle of Britain was won because there were enough people who, from 1935, believed it was coming and did not spare themselves in preparing for it. The night-bombing battle of the winter of 1940–41 was won because, in the early summer of 1940, the Air Staff, the R.A.F. Signals organization, Fighter Command, the radar scientists and, far from least, Tizard, all believed that it was coming and threw themselves into the task of preparation.

The essence of the night-defence problem was to provide the crew of a night fighter with continuous and accurate instructions from the ground as to the course to steer and the height to fly in order that a night fighter could approach an enemy bomber from astern to within a range which allowed the aircraft radar set in the fighter, the A.I. set, to be used. Any solution of the problem demanded a knowledge, *at one and the same point on the ground*, of the position, track, speed and height of both the enemy bomber and the night fighter. With this information, the controller on the ground is able, by radiotelephony, to tell the fighter the direction and height he should fly in order to intercept the enemy and, if necessary, tell the fighter when to slacken speed in order to avoid overshooting the bomber target. The solution of this problem was reached with what became known as the Plan Position Indicator, which was installed in a new form of radar set known as the G.C.I. (Ground Controlled Interception). To the controller of the interceptions, who needed to know little or nothing of the complications inside the radar boxes, the indications were the simplest yet achieved in any radar set. He had before him the screen of a cathode-ray tube, similar in size to that of a domestic television set. Marked permanently on this screen was a map of the surrounding area up to distances from him of about 50 miles. Positions of the hostile bomber and friendly fighter were shown by bright spots on the tube face; these spots were, in fact, small arcs of circles the centres of which it was the controller's business to estimate. As the bomber flew towards its target and as the fighter flew to intercept it, so the spots moved across the tube and the positions of the two aircraft could be read from the tube face which, in addition to the map, was marked in grid squares. These positions were plotted on a larger scale map and by calculating the speed and direction of flight of the enemy, the night fighter could be directed towards it by the shortest route. Friend was distinguished from foe by virtue of the I.F.F. set (Identification, Friend from Foe) carried on the night fighter which caused the friendly spot to give a characteristic signal every few seconds; it must, however, be admitted that this method of identification was not infallible.

Let us for a moment look at how this apparent miracle of modern science had come about. In pre-war days the radar scientists at Bawdsey had, largely because of fundamental advances made by the War Office team, evolved the C.H.L. set for locating low-flying aircraft. Because it used the then small wavelength of $1\frac{1}{2}$ m., it was possible to use a radar beam swinging over a large sector. This set was, however, a long way from being a Ground Controlled Interception set, but it was the starting-point from which a number of separate teams at Worth Matravers set about their various tasks. One team evolved an aerial system and mounting which produced a continuously rotating beam of the familiar lighthouse pattern. Another team attacked the all-important problem of determining the height of observed aircraft. Incidentally, one great advantage of controlling an interception direct from the radar station was that it was not the absolute position in space of the enemy and friendly aircraft that needed to be determined, but their relative positions; this simplified the problem. Another team worked upon a new method of display and evolved the first Plan Position Indicator in May 1940. In essence, it was a simple arrangement. As the aerial array rotated, so the radar beam rotated and, in alignment with it, a line from the centre of the radar screen to its circumference rotated so as to sweep over the whole area of the tube about every 20 seconds. This line was the range scale and its brilliance on the tube was kept at a low value. If, however, the rotating beam encountered an aircraft, a bright spot appeared on the rotating line and formed a small arc at the indicated range of the aircraft from the station. Since the direction of the rotating beam was at all times known, the direction of the located aircraft was also known. This was the Plan Position Indicator which, by the end of the war, was to be characteristic of modern radar on land, at sea and in the air.

Here then, after an unfruitful period, was a success at last. Later I shall seek to show that too many successes are apt to kill research Establishments but it is equally true that·they die if they have none. The evolution of the first Ground Controlled Interception set, in which W. B. Lewis, D. Taylor, F. C. Williams and many others played vital parts, not only raised the morale of A.M.R.E. but led to a close association between the operational users of night-fighter aircraft and the radar scientists. Had we stayed in Dundee it is substantially certain that a solution of the problem of night defence would not have been found in time for the Night Battle of Britain of the winter 1940–41, but at Swanage the stage was set for operational experiments which fascinated Service and scientific personnel alike during the summer of 1940. The first G.C.I. set had been built at Worth Matravers; Fighter Command arranged for the co-operation of a night-fighter squadron at Middle Wallop, where we were greatly helped by Flight-Lieutenant ('Cat's-eye') J. Cunningham, whose fame was yet to come. Not least, the enemy kindly sent sufficient bombing aircraft over our area to enable realistic experiments to be made. Except in bright moonlight, however, the help given by the G.C.I. set to the night fighters stopped at a crucial stage in the attempted interception. The G.C.I. set enabled a night fighter to be directed so that it was flying a mile or two behind the enemy, in more or less the same direction and at more or less the same height. The night fighter having been put in this position, a radar set in the night fighter itself (the A.I. set) was needed to enable the fighter crew to home on to the hostile bomber until it could be seen and engaged in battle. Before describing the first operational experiments at Worth Matravers it is therefore well to take stock of progress made with the A.I. set.

While the bulk of the research staff was settling into Worth Matravers, the airborne radar team, fortunately still under Bowen, was starting work at Christchurch aerodrome, near Bournemouth. The R.A.F. had there provided for us a detachment of aircraft and R.A.F. personnel to fly and maintain them. The chief task of this team was to develop an A.I. set for night-fighter aircraft. It may seem that progress with this first airborne radar set was slow in comparison with that of the ground radar installations which, in the spring of 1940, were ready and waiting for the enemy. No one would expect any project to be slow which had Bowen's dynamic energy behind it and, as part of my task of showing how radar research work was done, it is well to describe some of the difficulties of installing radar sets in aircraft. Much of what I have to say on this point will apply to the airborne radar work of the years to come.

There will always be a limit to the number of aircraft the R.A.F. can provide and (what is more difficult) maintain for experimental work and the wonder is that, during the lean times before and during the Battle of Britain, aircraft for experimental purposes were provided at all. There were, in fact, important voices which urged that all available aircraft should be thrown into the battle; had not wiser counsels prevailed, the airborne team would have been disbanded with consequences to the outcome of the war

PLATE III

T.R.E. AT WORTH MATRAVERS, 1940

beyond assessment. With few aircraft available for experimental work, it follows that there was a limit to the number of research staff that could be engaged on experimental flying work. A large-scale effort of the kind made on the coastal chain can rarely be made in the field of airborne radar. Another difference between ground and aircraft radar work is no less important. Within the limits of practical engineering, no one much minds what a ground radar set weighs; moreover it can usually be given all the electric power it needs and it usually has a country field, or the like, to itself. The aircraft radar designer, on the other hand, has to fight for every ounce of weight, every cubic inch of space and every pound of extra resistance to the aircraft's flight. Even when the principle is accepted that an aircraft must do something more than fly fast and high, the radar designer has to compete with those who design equipment to enable the aircraft to be flown and navigated; with those who have to instal bombs, guns and ammunition; with those who give aircraft the eyes of the modern aircraft camera; with those responsible for ordinary radio communications between ground and air; with those responsible for lighting and heating equipment and with those who have dozens of other and varied claims. All want weight, all want space and many want dispensations regarding increasing the resistance of the aircraft to flight and so lowering its speed. In the face of these long-established claims, the airborne radar team, new to the game, had to make its voice heard with promises rather than with tales of accomplished deeds. That the early airborne radar team was given a large measure of consideration and that the day came, years later, when there was much talk of designing aircraft round the radar sets, was less to the credit of the radar team, which naturally believed in its wares, than to the Air Staff and the Commands which, in the middle of a war, took great risks in assisting the

5-2

evolution of aircraft radar. This explanation of the difficulties of evolving aircraft radar must suffice for the rest of my story. It is however well to note that the German Air Force ruled with a harder rod the scientists who sought to serve them and that, even at the end of the war, German airborne radar was a negligible factor.

Under these conditions the airborne radar team continued at Christchurch and in the wooden huts of Worth Matravers a task which had been made difficult at Bawdsey because of the prior claims of the coastal chain, difficult at Perth because of the Scottish winter and difficult in South Wales because of separation from the main body of scientific workers. The chief objectives of the airborne radar team were the increase of maximum range, decrease of minimum range to a distance which provided a fighter pilot with a visual sight of his prey and, more generally, the evolution of an A.I. set capable of being used under Service conditions. In the summer of 1940 an A.I. set, known as Mark III, became operational in Blenheim aircraft. Its maximum range was two miles and its minimum range had been reduced to the still undesirably large value of 800 ft. The main trouble with the set was that its indication of directions for homing on to an enemy was not sufficiently accurate or consistent: not to put too fine a point upon it, the set was often 'squint-eyed'. In solving these problems, splendid assistance was given by the newly formed Fighter Interception Unit, under the command of Wing-Commander G. P. Chamberlain, primarily set up to study the tactical problems imposed by radar devices. Chamberlain was good for us in that he was not interested in what an A.I. set might do if a modification were made to it; he chose not to look beyond what the set was doing at a particular moment and place. Under operational conditions the difficulties with the slow Blenheim aircraft, fitted with Mark III A.I., were all too apparent during the late summer of 1940. There was no lack of incidents in which, with the aid of A.I., hostile aircraft were chased by our night fighters, but until the end of October 1940, only one enemy bomber had been destroyed with the aid of A.I. By the end of the summer of 1940 a great step forward had been made. With the aid of a great contribution made by Industry, a Mark IV A.I. set was evolved, with a maximum range of nearly four miles and a minimum range of only 600 ft. These sets were installed in the speedy Beaufighter aircraft and, with the G.C.I. sets, contributed greatly to the defeat of the German night bombers during the winter of 1940–41.

During that lovely summer of 1940 we often saw hostile day bombers flying over us. One day we counted seventy-two of them which, in passing us by, ignored our contribution to the war. There were times when, during paper bag lunches on the cliffs of St Alban's Head, I saw aircraft with smoking tails take their last dives into the sea. But these events were little concern of ours, for our eyes were on the coming night-bombing war. We had a G.C.I. set from which fighters could be controlled; we had the co-operation of A.I. fitted night fighters at Middle Wallop and we had of enemy night bombers enough for our purpose. These were the tools which helped us to a rebirth; this was when we began to live again. After our day's work many of us (too many for physical comfort) went to our G.C.I. station, hoping that this would be the night on which civilian scientists, working as controllers at a research Establishment, would be the means of bringing down a night bomber. In theory, it looked simple enough to us. All that was needed was for a night fighter to patrol up and down the English Channel until told by radiotelephony from the Worth Matravers G.C.I. station that there was an enemy in a suitable position for interception. Bomber and fighter would then be tracked and their heights assessed. When the fighter had been put on to the tail of the bomber by directions from the G.C.I. station, the latter would give the signal 'Flash Weapon' which would tell the fighter crew that the A.I. set should be switched on and used to complete the interception. The time was to come when it really was almost as simple as this, but not at Worth Matravers. In our innocence, we had thought that fighter aircraft were able to patrol the English Channel at night without losing their way, but this was not so. The first task was therefore to gain the confidence of the night-fighter pilots by using the G.C.I. indications to bring them from the English Channel to a position over their home aerodrome. Once this had been demonstrated, the fighter pilots poured over from Middle Wallop to see the new brand of magic, after which they came to believe that, though they might not know where they were, there was an 'eye' on the ground that could watch them and lead them home.

So it came about that scientists in flannel bags controlled night-fighter aircraft against the enemy. This was hardly a situation which could be tolerated for long and so a grey-haired pilot officer of the last war was appointed to see that civilian scientists did not make unreasonable demands on night-fighter crews: truth to tell, almost every demand seemed unreasonable to one who had fought in a pre-radar age but, thanks to Cunningham's grand backing and faith in us, the work went on.

It is sad to record that those who had evolved G.C.I. failed to obtain a kill before they were replaced by R.A.F. controllers who, in fact, did the job much better. Lack of immediate success was attributable partly to the use of Blenheim aircraft which often failed to overtake their prey; partly to the teething troubles of new equipment and a new operational method, and partly, perhaps, to the tendency of

70

scientists to be too much aware of the technicalities, too absorbed with signs of possible equipment failure, to make good controllers.

One G.C.I. set could not win a battle, nor a few A.I. sets. Moreover, Fighter Command had to effect a revolution in its methods of intercepting the enemy. In the early part of the war there was a tendency for Fighter Command H.Q. at Stanmore to exercise a somewhat rigid control of operations against day bombers, though, as the scale of the enemy effort increased, Group H.Q. and Sector H.Q. took more and more responsibility. Against day bombers, however, it was still true that attempts at interception were in the hands of fairly senior officers working in large and elaborately equipped control rooms. Night interceptions had, however, to be conducted from G.C.I. stations in which, in the early types, there was not room to swing a cat. In 1940 the day had not come when they were to be designed with bathrooms.

Following the success of the operational experiments at Worth Matravers it was clear that a great effort would be needed to provide sufficient ground and airborne radar equipment for the coming night battles. Fortunately nothing like the vast engineering complexities of the coastal chain were needed but instead of the years the latter had taken to build, we had only months. For the G.C.I. sets a 'crash programme' was started which aimed at twelve sets by the end of the year. Crash programmes, with which we became familiar as the war went on, are not easy to define but the idea behind them was that something for the R.A.F., however second best, should be produced as quickly as possible. Often it happened that sets were hand-made with odd bits and pieces and that some parts of an equipment were made before other parts had been developed. On 16 October 1940 the first of twelve G.C.I. sets was taken from Worth

Matravers, where it had been built, and installed at a selected site; on 18 October it was used in operations. By Christmas Day, six had been installed and the last of the twelve was ready on 6 January 1941. Similar intensive effort was made to produce sufficient A.I. sets to equip first Blenheim and then Beaufighter aircraft.

Now winter was with us and the efforts of the enemy to bomb our cities by night had begun and were increasing in scale. It would be pleasant to tell a story of how, on the availability of radar for night defence, the enemy's night bombers fell from the skies in large numbers, but it would not be a true story. Most will recall that, during the winter of 1940–41, the destruction of one night bomber was deemed worthy of a newspaper headline; the public was apprehensive, the R.A.F. was denied the stimulus of success and the radar scientists were bitterly disappointed. Yet from this disappointment lessons were learnt which were greatly to increase the speed with which the ideas of the radar scientists could be transformed into practical devices for the frustration of the enemy. What had caused the relative failure of the radar equipment was, on analysis, all too clear. Parts of the coastal chain for use against day bombers had been in existence for a number of years before they played their part in the Battle of Britain and there had been time to rectify faults and to train R.A.F. personnel to maintain and operate the equipment. The G.C.I. and A.I. sets were, however, thrown into the night battles without this vital period of assimilation. Clearly radar boxes were not enough; test gear had to be made, capable of being used under difficult conditions; R.A.F. personnel had to be speedily trained to use equipment in meagre supply and special means had to be provided for servicing hastily built equipment. These problems were attacked with vigour. Out of our troubles a new team was formed, under G. W. Dummer, for the sole purpose of designing synthetic training devices. Dummer's team evolved an A.I. trainer which simulated the appearance of the A.I. indications on a radar screen and enabled a night-fighter crew to practise homing on to an enemy bomber without leaving the ground. By the end of the war, training devices of this kind had played a vital part in the story of radar and had saved tens of thousands of hours of flight and over one million gallons of petrol. Thus, out of our troubles was born a new service to the R.A.F. Failures with the G.C.I. and A.I. equipment taught us, too, that we had to follow our devices out into the field and to assist in their maintenance until R.A.F. personnel could be trained to be self-sufficient. These new conceptions of our functions altered, almost imperceptibly at first, the character of our Establishment; they became in time of greater importance to the war than the evolution of new devices and they contained the seeds of the decline of the Establishment as a source of ideas.

With a knowledge of the causes of failure, remedies involving still closer co-operation between Service user and radar scientist were applied which soon led to success.

It is not my business to give an account of the air battles against the night bombers which took place in the winter of 1940–41 and continued until the following June; the story must be told by those who fought while, with a few exceptions, the scientists were asleep in their homes. But it is certainly a part of my story to relate the failures and successes of the scientists to the results of battle and none can doubt that a relationship exists. Before the radar scientists produced their devices and before R.A.F. personnel were trained to use them, the enemy's night-bomber losses were negligible. As usable devices were introduced, so the enemy losses increased month by month until, in May 1941,

73

102 enemy night bombers were shot down by fighters and 172 were assessed as probably destroyed or damaged.

During this period the casualty rate suffered by night bombers rose from less than half of 1 per cent to more than 7 per cent and the enemy attacks substantially ceased. This was victory indeed. It is true that on one or two brilliant moonlight nights the night fighters gained great victories over the enemy without much help from radar devices but on the darker nights radar proved indispensable. The night war of the air was the second major British victory of the war and, as with the first, victory depended upon radar. This second victory was achieved with the aid of a few G.C.I. sets and perhaps not more than 100 A.I. sets.

We at Worth Matravers gained much and learnt much from this period. We learnt how small a number of radar sets could sometimes make the difference between victory and defeat in a major battle; we learnt that we must follow our devices into the field and must, by designing training devices and in other ways, assist R.A.F. personnel to use the products of the scientists. The night-bomber battles had brought us into closer contact with operational crews who frequently visited A.M.R.E. and gave first-hand accounts of their experiences. Out of the heterogeneous collection of scientists and engineers who had collected at Worth Matravers in May 1940, teams were forming and morale was being built up after the doldrums of Dundee.

Perhaps more important than all else, this period saw the birth of the application of centimetre wavelengths to radar. It is my view that this event had a greater importance, and a greater grandeur, than any other event in the history of radar, in any country. It is well that it should have a chapter to itself.

CHAPTER IX

WORTH MATRAVERS AND THE BIRTH OF CENTIMETRE APPLICATIONS

I BELIEVE that almost every new advance in radar technique and almost every new radar device had its origin in a union between a user with a great and often desperate need and men in the laboratories who produced ideas and techniques to meet that need. In support of this belief I would like to be able to establish that the birth of centimetre radar applications, which was to have a far greater effect on the outcome of the war than any other technical advance, was wholly associated with a great need; but I am not sure. That an immediate application existed is not in doubt but I think it likely that an important psychological factor played a vital part. I am trying to show, as honestly as I can, how progress was made in the field of radar, and it is my belief that many of the senior scientists recruited from the Universities believed themselves professionally superior to the Government scientists of long standing. They were certainly not superior in applied science for most of them had yet to learn, and learn magnificently, that neither a technical idea nor a laboratory demonstration will win a battle. But that many of the newly recruited men were more gifted with the elusive quality of genius and professionally more competent in fundamental physics than most of the pre-war men, I have not the slightest doubt. What mattered was to assess the very different attributes of all members of the staff and to use them in the common task.

It is true that there were men, of whom Ratcliffe for the Air Ministry and Cockcroft for the War Office were conspicuous examples, who immediately and gladly threw themselves into known applications of radar, but there were others who at all costs wanted new fields in which to work. These men were accustomed, in their University work, to the task of wrestling with the secrets of nature without regard to possible applications and on joining us at Dundee or at Worth Matravers they sought, perhaps without knowing it, the most difficult work, and they sought novelty. In brief, I think it is likely that the subconscious reluctance of the newly recruited scientists to work on improvements in existing techniques was a factor in the birth of the application of centimetre wavelengths to radar.

There is however no doubt that a user-need, the need for an A.I. set on centimetre wavelengths, was the inspiration and the driving power behind the amazing progress made in the centimetre field.

The A.I. sets used in the night battles already described were far from perfect in their performance. It will be recalled from Chapter IV that the pre-war drive for radar on $1\frac{1}{2}$ m. was associated with the need for a radar beam, as distinct from floodlighting. A beam was certainly obtained with this wavelength but it was a wide beam and not at all like the beam we have seen all too often from an ordinary searchlight. In fact some of the energy from the aircraft A.I. transmitter was radiated straight downwards and the earth sent back a signal so vastly greater than any aircraft could do, that indications of an enemy aircraft at distances greater than the distance between the aircraft and the earth, i.e. greater than the height of the aircraft, were completely swamped. Thus the A.I. set fitted in a night fighter was unable to detect an enemy aircraft if the latter was at a greater distance than the height of the fighter

76

above the ground. If the fighter flew at 10,000 ft. it could, and usually did, observe a hostile bomber when about 10,000 ft. (or nearly two miles) away from it and this range sufficed for interception; if, however, a night bomber flew at a height of 2,000 ft. the night fighter naturally had to come down to intercept it at this height and, in doing so, its A.I. range was reduced to the seriously low value of 2,000 ft. In theory, the difficulty could have been overcome by having a formidable array of 1½ m. aerials fitted to a night fighter, so narrowing the beam; but an aircraft carrying this array would be an aircraft designer's nightmare. In practice, it was clear that the beam had to be narrowed to such an extent that the earth's reflections did not interfere with those from aircraft and it was no less clear that this could only be achieved with a wavelength of a few centimetres.

Another trouble with the 1½ m. A.I. set was that the indications it gave a night-fighter observer of the direction of a hostile bomber were not sufficiently accurate; the wonder was that failures to intercept from this cause were not more frequent. Again it was clear that the solution lay in narrowing the beam and this inevitably meant centimetre wavelengths.

A third factor responsible for the urge for A.I. on a wavelength of a few centimetres was the fear that the 1½ m. A.I. would be rendered useless by deliberate jamming.

With the emphasis put, in the summer of 1940, on the need for radar aids in the coming night battles, there was therefore no lack of incentive behind a drive for centimetre A.I. That for this first attempt to apply centimetre wavelengths to the war, the most difficult of all applications was chosen (whether for radar on land, sea or in the air) was not then known. Had it been appreciated, I think it likely that it would have provided the newly recruited scientists with a further reason for choosing this field of effort.

With a knowledge of the work being done on centimetre valves by Oliphant and J. T. Randall at Birmingham, some consideration was given at Dundee to the possibilities of using centimetre wavelengths, particularly by Robinson, Skinner and Ward who had newly joined the scientific staff. At that time the problem was also under review by Bowen, Lovell and Hodgkin at St Athan. We need not dwell on this phase of centimetre history because no facilities existed at Dundee or St Athan for work in the centimetre field. It is, of course, equally true that no facilities for the work existed at Worth Matravers in May 1940, but men had joined us who could provide the facilities and we at least had a magnificent site for experimental work.

The moving spirit behind the drive for an early application of centimetre radar was Dee. He was a nuclear physicist and not a radio specialist and it is therefore not surprising that at least one voice warned me almost daily of the folly of rushing into a centimetre application. But in applied science, and perhaps in much else, it is well to back a man with fire in his belly and I had no hesitation in giving Dee what help I could; it was little enough. Fortunately, we had the support of Sir Frank Smith, then Controller of Communications Equipment at the Ministry of Aircraft Production and of Watson-Watt, who had become Scientific Adviser on Telecommunications at the Air Ministry. To most others concerned we tended to minimize the effort being put into centimetres and the extent of our hopes.

The beginning was in May 1940 when Dee visited Oliphant at Birmingham. Oliphant had one type of equipment for generating power on a wavelength of about 10 cm.; it was known as a klystron. By means of a focusing mirror,

Oliphant had produced a narrow beam of the kind needed for an A.I. set, but we had better pause to see how very far Dee and his team had to go before even the crudest experimental A.I. set could be installed in an aircraft. The Oliphant klystron, with its power supplies, was a large piece of laboratory equipment which not even Dee and his team could conceive being installed in an aircraft; even so it developed a power of only one-fifth of a kilowatt. The Oliphant beam looked promising but its narrowness, so much desired, meant that arrangements would need to be made for it to sweep the skies. Moreover, methods for receiving the energy reflected from a target aircraft, and for using this energy to display the position of the target, had to be evolved. To undertake these gigantic tasks, at a time when Britain was far nearer defeat than victory, needed moral courage of a high order.

As a first step, Dee took Oliphant's drawings of a klystron to the Mond Laboratory, Cambridge, where a klystron was constructed (more as a private arrangement than anything else). In June 1940 this equipment arrived at Worth Matravers, but the look of it did nothing to encourage hope that the installation of centimetre wavelengths in aircraft was within sight; it even had its own pumping plant for creating the near-vacuum needed in the working space of the valve. This was however but the beginning. Soon Oliphant and his team produced a model of another type of generator of centimetre waves, a magnetron, which was sealed, i.e. the vacuum could be maintained without pumping plant. With this magnetron a useful power of about 5 kW. was obtained on a wavelength of 10 cm. The G.E.C. Research Laboratories under C. C. Paterson quickly developed a model of this valve suitable for production and experiments with it began at Worth Matravers in July 1940. These experiments were possible because, meanwhile, the problems associated with receiving centimetre wavelengths had been attacked by the Clarendon Laboratory at Oxford, and by Admiralty scientists. The whole of this work was co-ordinated by one of the most useful technical committees of the war, the Co-ordination of Valve Development Committee, where Government scientists of all three Services, scientists and engineers in Industry and Service users met to discuss programmes of valve development.

Now the fun began. When I review in my mind the war period, a few events stand out with such clarity that I can recall where I was sitting or standing at the time, what the weather was like and the tone of a voice that gave me my moment. One such was when I was asked on the telephone at Worth Matravers to see the 10 cm. equipment showing an echo from a man and his bicycle. For me, this was an even greater moment than when, in August 1940, reflections from a Battle aircraft at a range of two miles were got from the ground equipment at Worth Matravers.

These first experiments on the application of centimetre wavelengths to a war problem were destined to lead to a revolution in radar equipment for all three fighting Services. We had better pause a moment however to look at the Establishment as a whole, for the bulk of it was soon to move again, though this time not very far.

CHAPTER X

SWANAGE

AFTER the depressing conditions of Dundee, most of us
were happy at Worth Matravers. It is true that
instead of the imposing laboratories built for us at
Bawdsey we had temporary huts, not made more pleasant
by being surrounded by protective earthworks. But they
served their purpose and there was plenty of land and a cliff
site for field experiments. The Swanage landladies were
kind to the gradually increasing staff and the time was
yet to come when, with the removal of restrictions on
travel to the coast, many of them preferred holiday-makers
to radar scientists.

Curiously enough, I cannot recall clearly why we packed
much of our equipment and moved first into an empty
school, Leeson House, about half-way between Worth
Matravers and Swanage and then, with a more rapidly
increasing staff, also into another school, Durnford House.
This latter move was the first occasion on which we were
forced to dispossess a boys' school, but it was not to be the
last. I am fairly sure, however, that these relatively simple
moves were associated with the natural fear of Headquarters
that the Establishment at Worth Matravers would be a
target for air attack. Certainly we were conspicuous enough
with our 350 ft. and 240 ft. towers and much time was wasted
in air-raid shelters as hostile bombers passed over or near us.
There was, therefore, much to be said for moving most of the
equipment and personnel to less conspicuous quarters where
no notice need be taken of the persistent air-raid warnings,
and there was something to be said for dispersing the staff
providing that the constituent parts remained so close to one

another (within a mile or so) that the corporate life of the Establishment was not destroyed.

Once again the Air Ministry Works Department did great deeds for us in providing Leeson House with the heavy electric power supplies inseparable from our work. The school occupied a splendid site overlooking the town of Swanage and Swanage Bay, with a view of the Isle of Wight in the distance. This was an ideal location for the workers on centimetre wavelengths and soon there was a row of trailers, looking like caravans, each with a metal parabolic mirror overlooking the town and sea; this became known as 'Centimetre Alley' in which was done perhaps the most spectacular work in the whole history of radar. The astonishing successes of the radar scientists at Worth Matravers and at Leeson House were to have a major effect on the outcome of the war. The fresh fields of effort opened up during this period led to a fairly large increase of staff and soon we overflowed into Durnford House. Later, the need for a radar school led to the requisitioning of Forres School in Swanage. These four sections at Worth Matravers, Leeson House, Durnford and Forres worked as one Establishment during the Swanage era, an era which was to end in May 1942.

In November 1940, the Establishment changed its title for the last time and became known as T.R.E. The letters denoted Telecommunications Research Establishment, but for security reasons the full title was not used until the end of the German war. It was inevitable that a sense of mystery surrounded the meaning of the letters T.R.E. One member of the staff, not without cause, suggested that they meant Touring Round England.

It will have been noted that during the whole period from 1935 to the summer of 1940 the bulk of the work of the Establishment, wherever it was and whatever it was called, was directed to helping Fighter Command to defend Britain against the day and night attacks of hostile bombers. It follows that the invaluable and growing contacts between operational user and radar scientist were almost wholly confined to Fighter Command personnel. The Stanmore Operational Research Section under Larnder played a great part in keeping us in touch with the facts behind the many successes and occasional failures of Fighter Command. In the summer of 1940 this was still the only Command to have an Operational Research Section. It was, however, obvious that the war could not be won by defending this country from air attack. There was still the submarine to be defeated and, if this were achieved, there remained the gigantic task of carrying the war into the heart of Germany and of destroying her ability and will to continue the war.

It is not my purpose to catalogue the successes of the radar scientists, but rather to give a picture of the life of the men who achieved them and of the structure and character of the Establishment in which they worked. Many of the characteristics of T.R.E., which were later the subject of admiration, criticism or mirth, were born in the Swanage era, and before showing how radar devices spread into Coastal and Bomber Commands it seems well to give a picture of the special features which were characteristic of T.R.E. until the end of the war.

Important amongst these were our 'Sunday Soviets', which were later to achieve some publicity in the press. By the end of the war, Sunday meetings in my office had been attended by Cabinet Ministers, Tizard, Commanders-in-Chief, Air Marshals, Admirals and Generals, University professors, Service personnel straight from the heat of battle, those who controlled our destinies from Headquarters and, not least, scientists working in or alongside the laboratories.

6-2

Air Chief-Marshal Sir Philip Joubert's remark, 'You can say anything in Rowe's office on a Sunday', came to be quoted as the excuse, or reason, for the frankest exchanges of views on the progress of the war, and on means whereby radar might aid the work of the fighting men. I do not pretend that these Sunday meetings were universally popular or that there were not some who viewed them with distaste, but there is no doubt that the support for them was sufficient to produce a profound effect on many phases of the air war.

How did these curious Sunday meetings come about? Like radar itself, they were not born in a flash of inspiration but, again like radar, an idea played its part, and the rest was the will to follow up a relatively modest conception. In dealing with the birth of operational research I have said that, to me, the union of the Service user and the scientist was of paramount importance. It is my belief that this tenet, and one other (the sea war), were the only 'bees in my bonnet' during the war, though I may well be told that I had less fruitful ones as well.

During the period of stagnation at Dundee I had tried to cheer things up by inviting distinguished serving officers and others to visit Dundee for 'free-for-all' discussions. Nothing much happened because the air war had not begun in earnest, and perhaps because we had so little to give.

The next step in the birth of Sunday Soviets arose from a consideration of the number of days we should work each week. At Dundee we accepted the biblical dictum and rested on Sundays. After the German onslaught of May 1940 we, then at Swanage, began to work seven days each week, but it was soon clear that the best scientific work was not to be done in this way. We then tried a scheme in which each member of the staff, in theory, took a day's rest each week, the choice of the day being left to the individual. This did not work, partly because it was inconvenient and partly because many of the scientists never seemed to find a suitable day.

I therefore decided, with Headquarters' approval, to close the Establishment for one day each week. Meanwhile, out of the troubles of others, there arose a fortunate circumstance for us. The strain on senior R.A.F. officers and on senior civilians in London, imposed by their heavy tasks and by the efforts of the Germans to rob them of sleep, led them to seek a change of air on Sundays when the tension of their lives tended to slacken. Many of them sought relaxation at Swanage, not least of them Joubert, who lived nearby.

Gradually a large Swanage hotel became accustomed to its uniformed clientele of high and not-so-high rank, who found that on Sundays they could help us, learn from us and get some sleep and fresh air at the same time. More than once, in later years, I was told by distinguished visitors that the strain of taking part in a Sunday Soviet was greater than that imposed by any other of their weekly tasks; but, in the early Swanage days, there was a little of the holiday atmosphere about the Sunday Soviets which did much to foster friendships and maintain relative sanity.

Having decided, therefore, to close T.R.E. one day each week, it was clear that Sunday was the last day to choose; and so it happened that Saturday was chosen for our rest day, and remained so until the end of the German war.

I have thought it important to describe the intentional and accidental factors which played their part in the birth of Sunday Soviets, from which so much was to come, partly because I believe that a vital part of creating any organization is to take advantage of fortuitous circumstances. In 1942 we took our habit of Sunday working and Saturday rest with us to a distant county where it was commonly assumed that the personnel of the newly-arrived Establishment was exclusively of the Jewish faith.

85

But why were our Sunday meetings called Soviets? Just before the war began, a distinguished visitor from another Government department attended one of our somewhat noisy meetings at Bawdsey and, in critical vein, referred to the freedom of speech which prevailed. 'Just like a Soviet', he said. It was a good enough description.

When I became Superintendent at Bawdsey in 1938 we had a handful of drawing office staff and about 20 mechanics working at the Establishment. By the end of the war our drawing office strength was nearly 200 and we had one of the finest model shops in the country, employing about 500 men of various trades. A growth of this kind could not fail to affect the character of T.R.E., and we had better see how it came about.

Of course, radar scientists, like most others, need a few highly skilled instrument makers and turners to make single items of experimental equipment for use in the laboratories, but no body of research workers at a University has or needs a large drawing office and a workshop of factory dimensions to help them in their experiments.

In time of peace, the evolution of a complicated mechanical device, such as a new form of bombsight, takes about five years from the beginning of research upon it to the stage of its large-scale availability to the R.A.F. Because, in general, more latitude can be allowed in the design of an electrical than a mechanical device, the corresponding time for a radar device might be three or four years.

The changing character of T.R.E. as the war progressed will not be understood without some appreciation of how these years of evolution are spent, and of how short-circuiting action will sometimes greatly accelerate the availability of a device to the user. We will take as an example a radar device which it is intended should be installed in hundreds or even thousands of aircraft, perhaps of different types. First the research team evolves a model for tests in an aircraft set aside for experimental work. All that is asked of the model is that it shall be sufficiently robust not to catch fire or cause other trouble in the air and that it shall give something like the performance and indications which its designers intended. The aircraft will probably have had to be modified to take the experimental equipment. The time needed for the pre-liminary air experiments cannot be assessed, but they will usually occupy months. Unsuitable flying conditions may cause delay for a month or more, and a frustrated scientist may not do a single air experiment in this period.

After a series of experiments the application research team may be dissatisfied and may call for aid from basic research groups at the Establishment. The best that it can hope for is that the device works well enough for it to be shown to selected members of the R.A.F.; these may be R.A.F. personnel stationed at the aerodrome associated with the Establishment or at special units set up by the R.A.F., and, in addition, they may be R.A.F. officers of high rank specially interested in the device being tested. For example, towards the end of the war Air Vice-Marshal Bennett, the leader of Bomber Command's Pathfinder Force, frequently flew down from his Headquarters to test a device in its early research stage. Not every R.A.F. user, however, was able to visualize what the set might do when its teething troubles and crudities had been eliminated.

If the experimental set gave promising results we were then at the end of the beginning. A tidier set was usually built, and drawings in some detail were made of every unit com-prising the device. Meanwhile, there would already have been discussions between R.A.F. and civilian authorities at Headquarters, representatives of the user Command and the civilian scientists, on whether the project should continue and, if so, with what priority over other work; these discussions were frequently held at the Sunday Soviets. Much more difficult were the discussions on where the set was to be installed in different types of aircraft and on whether it would go in at all. Considerable modifications to the aircraft's structure were often demanded, which delayed aircraft production and drew understandable protests from the aircraft industry. Other installations in the aircraft had to be moved or eliminated, and those interested in them naturally joined the protestants. Usually a mock-up of the part of the aircraft concerned had to be built, in which dummy boxes were moved from place to place until an acceptable installation had been agreed upon. The Ministry of Aircraft Production department responsible for satisfying all claimants for space, weight and position of installation had surely one of the most difficult tasks of the war.

When T.R.E.'s drawings of the device were ready they were sent to the firm selected to manufacture it, though already there would have been preliminary discussions between representatives of the firm and of the Establishment. The firm is then usually faced with two tasks. One is to build a few sets so that more extensive trials can be conducted by the R.A.F., sometimes in actual operations, in which the need for modifications can be foreseen before large-scale production begins. No large firm likes doing this because the making of a few sets uses, almost exclusively, precious highly skilled workers. The firm's other task is to 'tool up' for production, which means the design and manufacture of jigs and tools which will enable hundreds and perhaps thousands of sets to be made by less highly skilled labour; otherwise, there would hardly be enough highly skilled labour in the country to manufacture more than two or three devices on a large scale. This stage in the evolution of the device takes several months, much to the disgust of the laboratory scientist. However, there is little difficulty in understanding how the time is spent. The drawings made at the Establishment are usually indispensable, but fresh drawings have to be made by the firm. The laboratory scientists can make one or two sets which give the required performance but, with few exceptions, they have not the engineering skill to produce designs suitable for manufacture. Even if they had, a firm will usually need to design the equipment in accordance with its chosen methods of manufacture and to suit the production plant at its disposal.

Meanwhile, the firm will have produced what is known as a manufacturers' prototype, which is a model of what the device will look like and a sample of how it will perform when it has been produced in large quantity. It is the responsibility of the research Establishment to test this model, and, again, serious delays may occur because of bad weather. When the tests are made it may be found that modifications are needed. It is not unlikely that the research team will meanwhile have found how to improve the performance of the device, and there will be a tussle between the scientists with their natural desire that only their best efforts should be used against the enemy and those who want something, even a second best, as soon as possible. Compromises are usually reached and the firm is told to proceed with manufacture.

At last sets begin to come from the firm, and a difficult decision may then confront the R.A.F. authorities responsible for giving instructions that the equipment is to be used against the enemy. It may well be that a few sets could usefully be used against the enemy at once, but if this involves sending them over enemy territory, with a grave risk of capture, a serious problem arises. Capture of the set means that the enemy will have time to prepare against its use on a large scale, and perhaps to counter it; it means, too, that the enemy can, if it suits his plans, take the benefit of our research and design efforts and manufacture the set for use against us. More important than any other factor, it means demonstrating to the enemy that the weapon can be achieved. For these reasons it may be decided to postpone using the device against the enemy until sufficient have been made to produce important results. If however the device is to be used over home territory, and if R.A.F. operational personnel have been trained in its use, and suitable test gear has been designed and built and arrangements made for servicing the device under the practical conditions of its use, then it will probably be decided to use sets as they become available from the firm. If the demand for the set is urgent and large numbers are needed quickly, other firms may be asked to manufacture, and again there are calls on the research Establishment to aid these firms.

If this account of the evolution of a radar device sounds unexciting, it is well that it should be so if I am to fulfil my purpose of showing a radar research Establishment at work. At the birth of a device there is plenty of excitement. A crude equipment made, as we used to say, of 'string and sealing wax' can be used to demonstrate to high-ranking R.A.F. officers that some great war need can probably be met. At these demonstrations every one is happy. The research workers are happy because they have demonstrated an effect of vast import, and the high-ranking officers are happy because they see a light where there was none. Then, however, comes the long grind over the months and probably years before the device contributes to the defeat of the enemy.

There was plenty of excitement, in fact, in discovering through the years how to shorten the period between the birth of an idea and its full-scale use in operations. We recruited more and more skilled mechanics who co-operated with the scientists in the task of improving the engineering features of a design, so relieving industry of part of its great burden. We learnt how to make our drawings more acceptable to the firms, again easing their load; and, finally, we acquired facilities which often enabled us to manufacture a few sets ourselves. While industry was studying the new device and preparing for manufacture, these sets were used for preliminary trials, for training R.A.F. personnel and sometimes on operations.

The birth of this attack on the time factor occurred towards the end of our stay in Swanage, though intensification of the attack and the fruits thereof were to come when we had moved elsewhere. We had already established a drawing office, some small workshops serving groups of laboratories and a larger workshop for general work. What we now needed was a model shop properly equipped for small-scale production. This involved a heavier demand on skilled labour than we had hitherto faced, and it was decided to build the semi-factory near a source of living accommodation greater than was offered by Swanage. A site was found at West Howe, near Bournemouth, and work began there without a sign that our days in Swanage were numbered and that soon West Howe would be at an impracticable distance from T.R.E. The future Engineering Unit had however been born.

Although almost every radar device for the R.A.F. was conceived in the laboratories of T.R.E., it must not be supposed that the steps which led to a progressive shortening of the period of evolution of a device were proposed only, or even chiefly, by members of the Establishment. We learnt from the accusations and suggestions of the staffs of the radio firms; in particular, we were greatly aided by Walter Symes of Metropolitan Vickers Limited. We had at Headquarters two successive Directors of Radio Production (Air Commodore H. Leedham and F. Tomlinson) who knew both the needs of industry and our own difficulties. Much was learnt from them. In 1943 Air Commodore Gregory, the first A.O.C. 60 Group R.A.F., retired from the Service and joined us to take charge of the engineering facilities of T.R.E., and the scientists owe much to him, also.

But, wherever credit lies, there is no doubt that there was born at Swanage an idea which later was to reduce to reasonable proportions the time taken to evolve a radar device. Much of the failure of the Germans to employ radar in aircraft is associated, in my view, with lack of an imaginative attack on some of the problems I have described. Some of the speed with which, towards the end of the war, the Americans brought new radar devices into action was associated with their appreciation of what had been done at T.R.E. In 1943 a distinguished American said to me: 'I want to know how you people get your stuff into the war so quickly.' I showed him the extent of the engineering and flying facilities which we then had, and he said: 'This is the answer. I need not look further.'

A horse, it has been said, can be taken to the water but not made to drink. It is almost equally true that a new device may be installed in an aircraft but, unless the crew believes in it, it might as well not be fitted. Their attitude to a new device is understandable. In the middle, perhaps, of an arduous and dangerous period of operations, members of the crew are given another gadget to learn about, another gadget to watch and to report upon at the end of each flight. If the importance of the device is not understood by the crew it is hardly likely to be properly used and, even if the crew is super-humanly conscientious, early troubles with an unfledged device may lead a crew to denounce the device in particular and scientists in general.

The remedy is simple enough. Rather than let crews receive an unheralded device with a cry of dismay, they should be told what is coming, why it is coming and be encouraged to grumble at the delay in its installation in their aircraft.

One method of achieving this spirit of anticipation in the squadrons has already been mentioned. Electronic training devices were evolved which simulated, as far as possible, the behaviour of the device in operation. By this means it was possible for an operational crew to become accustomed to using the device and to sense its importance without even having seen one.

Another method, which began at Swanage, was the making of talking films which showed potential users what a new device looked like, how to operate it and the kind of operational results which might be obtained from it. For example, an early A.I. film concluded, to the accompaniment of music, with a picture of a night bomber being shot down with the aid of this radar device. These films did much to encourage R.A.F. squadrons to want the equipment and to regard it as a friend when it came. Of course, the educative value of films was appreciated long before radar was born. While wondering at Dundee how we might help the training of radar crews at the coastal chain stations, I remembered seeing, in the early 1930's, a travelling cinema van in the village of Orford. The talking film told the villagers simply and clearly how they should vote in the next election, and why. As a direct result of this recollection I sought authority to recruit a man skilled in the making of films, as the result of which A. D. Segaller joined us at Dundee just before we left for Swanage. Special facilities for film making were provided at Swanage and I was delighted with my idea of making radar training films until I had a striking demonstration of my lack of originality. It became clear that I had been ignorant of the fact that a films branch existed at the Air Ministry for the sole purpose of making films. This branch rose in its wrath and demanded that we show cause why we should make our own films. A compromise was reached whereby we, who knew what was wanted, should do the photography and, with the aid of the R.A.F. users, write the script, but that much of the film production should be done elsewhere.

Thus began our film unit which, by the end of the war, had helped to make films dealing with most radar devices. Golden voices, such as that of John Snagge, were eventually used. Colour helped to provide realism and by the end of the war our films were regarded as a show-piece for visitors. The aim was to produce a film before the device which formed its subject became operational, and we sometimes succeeded.

In Chapter VIII I have referred to the early failure of the A.I. equipment to achieve results and to our realization that our task was not simply to evolve equipment but to help the R.A.F. to use it. Early in the war the R.A.F. set up its own radar schools, and it was natural that the instructors at these schools should frequently visit Swanage to see what was coming next. I cannot recall how it came about that T.R.E. started its own radar school with courses on various radar devices, possibly because it was a humble affair at the beginning and none could have known that it would grow to be one of the major features of the Establishment. Starting in a single hut, with L. G. H. Huxley as the sole lecturer, the school grew until, still under Huxley, it had a considerable teaching staff, and the civilian and Service personnel passing through the school were numbered in their thousands. Highlights in the school's history may serve to indicate the service it rendered to the R.A.F. and, to a smaller extent, to the other fighting Services.

The R.A.F. Senior Navigators' Course attended the school. Air Marshal Sir William Barrett, when A.O.C.

Training Command, said that if the rest of the Establishment did not exist, the school would be well worth visiting. A lasting impression I have of the school in its later years is a picture of a front row of Air Vice-Marshals and Air Commodores sitting at the feet of a succession of flannel-bagged lecturers. I remember feeling glad that this could not have happened in Germany.

One other general service to the R.A.F., born at Swanage, remains to be described; one which grew until the scientific staff it absorbed was larger than that in any other field of the Establishment's effort. Its birth came directly from the evolution of the first application of centimetre wavelengths to the needs of the R.A.F., the 10 cm. A.I. project, and the reasons for its birth are of considerable importance.

It must not be supposed that at the beginning of the war the civilian scientists had a monopoly of knowledge of radar. With the birth of radar, the excellent R.A.F. Signals organization, first under Air Vice-Marshal Nutting and later under Air Vice-Marshal Tait, had not been slow to provide its Signals personnel with sufficient knowledge of radar to ensure the proper maintenance of Service equipment. As long as radar was confined to wavelengths of metres, no difficulty arose because the techniques were not very different from those applicable to radio devices with which the Signals organization had been long familiar. With the coming of centimetre wavelengths, however, the position was entirely different. If, on the first day of the war, every single civilian scientist had been blotted out of existence, I do not doubt that the Battle of Britain would still have been won with the aid of radar. If, however, every single radar scientist knowledgeable on centimetre techniques had been similarly eliminated in 1940, the war would certainly have taken a different course. For the first time, the scientists had a monopoly of knowledge which, incidentally, did much to increase the prestige of scientists in the eyes of the Services. It was clearly not only in the interests of the war but in the interests of the designers of centimetre equipment to end this monopoly as soon as possible. If those with a flair for evolving centimetre devices had to follow the children of their imagination into the squadrons, to analyse set failures and to assist maintenance, there would be no more centimetre devices.

With the advent of centimetre A.I., therefore, we were faced with a major problem. We needed men whose task it was, not to originate devices but to study their behaviour under Service conditions; men capable, by virtue of a scientific training, of analysing the types of failure experienced in particular equipments under various conditions of use, of suggesting remedies and, not least, men capable of living with Service personnel at squadrons and of working and jesting with them. Above all we needed a leader for the work, one who was a first-class scientist and a first-class organizer. The combination is less rare than is commonly supposed, but the two attributes do not always go together. It was Dee who suggested Ratcliffe. Ratcliffe had been loosely attached to us at Dundee, but had later founded the radar school for the Army at Petersham. I appealed to Ratcliffe to rejoin us to undertake the task of building up a Post-Design Service. He came, and stayed until his scientific staff numbered hundreds, divided into groups for aiding the various R.A.F. Commands.

This P.D.S. work was of outstanding importance to the R.A.F. and to the scientists in the laboratories. As the war progressed the operational research sections at R.A.F. Commands inevitably and rightly extended their activities far beyond radar, and we came to rely on our P.D.S. staff for information on operations involving our equipment, rather than on the operational research staffs.

Without P.D.S. much of the work of the laboratory scientists would have been in vain.

Before continuing my story of the evolution of radar devices which were to prove indispensable to the winning of defensive and offensive battles in the air and at sea, I have tried to show something of the shape T.R.E. at Swanage was gradually taking and something of the features which came to be characteristic of it. But what most puts a stamp upon a research Establishment and gives it colour is not its special organizational features but the kind of people it possesses at the upper levels of its structure. These in turn will mould, for a time at any rate, the more junior members of the staff; and so an Establishment, if it is alive at all, will come to have a reputation, a colour, for good or ill. It must not however be supposed that during the formative years at Swanage T.R.E. was being moulded into a pattern dictated by its Head or, indeed, by anyone. On the contrary, a conscious effort was made to promote to high status men of very different attributes and temperaments. It may be thought that this policy was hardly conducive to peace and quiet; nor was it, for the verbal battles on what should be done and should not be done rolled on throughout the years of war.

Yet there were two attributes that had to be possessed by any member of T.R.E. before he was chosen for one of the highest posts. One was a fervent belief, a faith, that only by the full development and use of radar could the war be won. The other was the acceptance of the dictum of Moses's father-in-law that chosen leaders should be 'able men, men of truth, lacking covetousness'. We had no use for careerists. No one at T.R.E. was left in doubt that a camel's passage through the eye of a needle was easier than promotion to high status without the possession, in more than average measure, of these two attributes. Little of holy quiet resulted from this method of selection, but a body of leaders of different qualities and temperaments was gradually formed, which possessed in common a belief that by allowing the utmost freedom of expression on our own affairs, and often on those of others, the best paths to take would eventually be clear to all.

I have tried to stress that a powerful factor in the progress of radar was the splendid co-operation between the R.A.F. user and the civilian scientist. The understanding between members of these two totally different professions reached its zenith during the dangerous years of the war and may never again be achieved. It may well be wondered how it was possible for the two professions to work so well together. There are times when I can hardly believe it happened. Men who adopt one of the fighting Services as a profession are trained from youth to believe that loyalty and discipline, in capital letters, are the great cardinal virtues. The praises of the men who took part in the frivolous cavalry charge of Balaclava have been sung because they accepted that it was 'Theirs not to reason why'. The significance attached to examples of deliberate disobedience, such as that involving Nelson's blind eye, serves only to illustrate the rarity of these events. The need for a rigid standard of loyalty and discipline in the fighting Services is obvious, even to one who, like myself, prefers the civilian ways of life. If Bomber Command orders a bombing operation against Berlin, it cannot allow the bomber crews to argue that the war situation demands the bombing of oil installations or of docks. A decision on whether a Battle Fleet should engage the enemy at once, or wait for a more favourable opportunity, may have to be taken within minutes. If every ship of the Fleet were allowed to put the pros and cons of attack and withdrawal, chaos would result and the battle would be lost in any case. All this is obvious, but the same arguments do not apply at a research Establishment or among scientists who control research work from Headquarters. Of course, in any large research Establishment there must be a high and accepted standard of law and order in matters such as finance, the safeguarding of Government property and, for defence research, the preservation of secrecy. It was in matters of this kind that I used my rarely exercised 'right' of twelve casting votes at meetings of the twelve senior members of the Establishment. On most subjects, however, freedom of discussion can alone attract the right men to accept leadership, and from free discussions between men of ability and good will the best action to take is usually made clear to all. In an atmosphere of this kind, talk of loyalty and discipline has little place, though these attributes are usually present as ordinary courtesies of life. I do not suggest that every senior R.A.F. officer with whom we had contact or, indeed, every civilian understood our brand of democracy; there were no doubt some who would have welcomed the sight of temperamental scientists being drilled on a parade ground. But, in fact, we evolved a method of building and maintaining a team of the largest number of first-rate physicists ever to work together in this country. Our methods were accepted by the great majority of those with whom we came in contact, Service and civilian alike, perhaps because they produced results.

It is time to return to the story of the evolution of radar devices for the R.A.F. but I have thought it useful, in this chapter, to give an account of some of the characteristics of T.R.E. In what follows it is well to remember that the excitement of a new idea, and of the first experimental indications that a great need could probably be met, was but the prelude to a long and heavy task involving the design of the equipment, its installation in an operational aircraft, co-operation with industry, the design of test equipment, the making of a film, the training of R.A.F. users and the absorption of more of the Establishment's staff in the task of following the equipment into the Service.

It is well to remember, too, that I am but describing the activities of one Establishment. Volumes could be written of the parts played by Service and civilian authorities at Headquarters and by the British Radio Industry, but this is a task for the official historian.

CHAPTER XI

SWANAGE AND COASTAL COMMAND

IT is likely that, throughout the war, every thinking man or woman, whether Service or civilian, whether a Cabinet Minister possessing inner knowledge or a man-in-the-street possessing none, had a pet theory of how to prevent defeat or to achieve victory. My own view was that at all costs we had to win the war at sea against the enemy submarines. I do not suggest that this attitude of mind was right or wrong; I merely record it. To me, air battles over Britain were not associated with the fear of defeat. When France fell, what most worried me was not the defeat of our armies but the possession by the enemy of Atlantic ports in the Bay of Biscay. As the war went on, I was unable to see how Europe could ever be liberated by the allied armies until the seas were substantially clear of submarines, so that vast armies and their equipment could flow from the United States.

By the early summer of 1940, radar had done little to assist Coastal Command in a problem which, judging only by the extent of shipping losses, was not acute. At that time the enemy possessed relatively few submarines and there was no sign of the appalling shipping losses which were to result from the loss of the Biscay ports. Thus high priority was not given to the $1\frac{1}{2}$ m. A.S.V. project and the airborne radar group concentrated upon $1\frac{1}{2}$ m. A.I. None the less, some progress was made with the A.S.V. project and, with the fall of France, it received an added impetus. A number of Whitley aircraft were fitted with aerials which transmitted lobes of radiation, one in a direction about 25° to the left and the other about 25° to the right of the direction of flight. By continuously and rapidly switching the transmission from one aerial to the other, an indication was received of whether a ship or a submarine was to the left or the right of the fore and aft axis of the aircraft and, by altering course, the aircraft could be homed on to the vessel. This radar device had a maximum range of about four miles for surface submarine detection and for general sea reconnaissance the area swept per hour of patrol was small. It was found, however, that there was an immediate and vital use for this homing device. Because of unsolved navigational problems, Coastal Command aircraft had great difficulty in locating convoys which they had been ordered to protect against submarine attack; in poor visibility the task was almost hopeless. With A.S.V., however, a convoy could be homed on from ranges which often exceeded 30 miles. This was possible because convoys presented far greater reflecting surfaces than submarines. Thus aircraft were able to find a convoy and then use A.S.V. to search the surrounding area for submarines.

The first recorded submarine 'kill' with the use of A.S.V. was on 20 November 1941 and a useful toll continued to be taken of the enemy's relatively small but growing submarine fleet. It was however clear that when the enemy had time to develop submarine bases in the Bay of Biscay ports, the problem would become vastly more difficult. Yet it was here, in the Bay of Biscay, that in 1943 the German Submarine Fleet met disaster from which it was not to recover; a disaster which Hitler was gracious enough to attribute to a single technical invention, a type of A.S.V. not contemplated in 1940. The concentration of German submarines in the Bay of Biscay meant that the vessels had to make the passage of the Bay before they could operate against our shipping, and they had to get back again. Until the war was nearing its end, the need for submarines to charge their batteries compelled them to take the risk of making part of the passage of the Bay on the surface, thus presenting Coastal Command with a chance of destroying them. But it must be admitted that the chances of destroying a submarine were, at that time, not large. If a submarine commander considered surfacing in daylight to be too dangerous there was nothing to prevent his surfacing at night. Even if a submarine were located and homed upon in darkness, the difficulty of seeing it and delivering an accurate attack upon it was still great. The difference between the use of A.I. against a night bomber and the use of A.S.V. against a submarine is worth noting. In the former case, an A.I. set allows a night fighter to settle down behind an unsuspecting enemy bomber and the fighter pilot can usually choose his moment for opening fire. The task of a submarine-hunting aircraft is far more difficult. If it is to be successful, its crew must drop a bomb or depth charge with great accuracy, in the darkness, against an object only fleetingly seen in their rapid passage over it. Well may the crew remember a famous advertisement and say: 'That's a submarine, that was.' Still, a sunken submarine was not the only thing and great importance was attached to making these vessels dive as often as possible, thus striking at the morale of their crews, and hindering them in their attacks upon convoys.

Ranges of more than four miles were, however, badly needed and, in an effort to increase the range of location of submarines, a few Wellington aircraft were fitted with aerial arrays which were a nightmare to the aircraft designer. Along each side of the fuselage was installed a number of aerials which allowed a fairly wide beam to be radiated at right angles to the direction of flight, i.e. on the port and starboard beam of the aircraft. The appearance of the aircraft was not improved by the addition of homing aerials. Aircraft so fitted played a useful part in the battle against the submarines, but it was becoming increasingly clear that the submarine problem was not likely to be solved with $1\frac{1}{2}$ m. radar. The methods of display, particularly with the beam aerials, demanded of radar operators an almost superhuman degree of concentration. Several flights of several hours each might be made in miserable flying conditions without a submarine being sighted; yet the operators had constantly to maintain the high degree of awareness demanded by the transient nature of a none too clear indication of the presence of a submarine. What was needed was a radar map of the surrounding ocean on which would appear an indication of any surface object within range. In June 1941, we proposed to Headquarters that work should begin on an A.S.V. set using centimetre wavelengths and approval was obtained in the same month. In principle, the scheme was simple. A very narrow beam, obtainable with centimetre wavelengths, was to rotate continuously so as to scan the surface of the sea. An object on the surface, such as a submarine, would show as a bright spot on a cathode-ray tube and the position of the spot on the tube would give the range and bearing of the target. The importance of such a simple method of display in an aircraft cannot be overestimated. Work began at Swanage but was to come to fruition elsewhere.

The use of centimetre wavelengths for submarine location had, however, an earlier origin in one of the most significant demonstrations ever given at T.R.E. In November 1940 Naval officers and civilian scientists belonging to the Admiralty Signals Establishment were invited to witness the detection of a submarine in Swanage Bay, using a 10 cm. radar set in 'Centimetre Alley' at Leeson House. The result justified the fervent beliefs of Dee, Skinner and others in centimetre wavelengths. Thus it came about that T.R.E. was the cause of the introduction of 10 cm. radar into the Navy. Lest it be thought that virtue was the monopoly of one Establishment, let it be remembered that the Admiralty was largely responsible for the availability of centimetre valves and that our part was to urge an application to the needs of the Navy. Let it be remembered, too, that the Navy was the first Service to use 10 cm. radar operationally, though all would admit that installation in ships was a far easier task than installation in aircraft.

I have said that it was the war at sea which was the greatest source of anxiety to me, not so much in my capacity as Head of the Establishment but as a citizen who was interested in being on the winning side. I trust that my many friends in the R.A.F. have forgiven me for pestering them on the subject. One of our troubles at Swanage was that we did not know what was happening in the battles against the submarines, largely because there was nothing at Coastal Command corresponding to the Operational Research Section at Fighter Command. We wanted to know the hours flown per submarine sighting by day and by night, the average ranges of radar locations and, less obviously our business, the results of attacks on submarines. I therefore went to Air Marshal Sir Wilfred Freeman, Vice-Chief of the Air Staff, who was ever ready to listen, and urged that P. M. S. Blackett should be asked to form an Operational Research Section at Coastal Command. This was arranged within a few days.

As, unknown to us, our days at Swanage drew to an end, the position of the war against the German submarine fleet was not good. Shipping losses were heavy and submarines were not greatly hindered in their passage through the Bay. Radar on 1½ m. had grave limitations for submarine hunting and progress with centimetre A.S.V. was retarded by the higher priority given to the needs of Fighter and Bomber Commands.

Still graver days were to come before, far from Swanage, T.R.E. evolved the decisive weapon which enabled Coastal Command, in co-operation with the Navy, to defeat the menace of the submarine.

CHAPTER XII

SWANAGE AND BOMBER COMMAND

I N the early days of Swanage there was no sign that, by the end of the war, T.R.E. would have spent more effort on Bomber Command than on any other Command. In 1940 there was little talk among radar scientists about the problems of bombing Germany. The force available for a bombing offensive was very small and, because all thoughts were on the dire needs of defence, no appeal was made to the radar scientists to come to the aid of Bomber Command.

It is probably true that no one foresaw the appalling difficulties confronting a sustained and successful bombing offensive against Germany; certainly no whisper of these difficulties had reached us by mid-1940. Because it is my aim to show how and when radar needs were born and met, it is important to consider why, in the pre-war years, the Air Staff and Fighter Command were aware of the deficiencies of their plans for air defence and why they seized instantly on the hope of radar, while the Air Staff and Bomber Command were not similarly alarmed about the efficacy of air bombing. In questions of this kind it is always easy to suggest that in one field of effort men were alive and in the other they were dead, but in my experience it is more profitable to look elsewhere for a solution and in this case one is not hard to find. Even in pre-war days, Fighter Command was able to conduct exercises over this country in which the Observer Corps, sound locators and searchlights were used for locating aircraft simulating raids on our cities and in which fighter aircraft sought to intercept the 'enemy'. It was as a result of exercises of this kind that the need for revolutionary air-defence methods was disclosed.

When radar had provided this revolution, exercises went on under conditions which were, for the fighter aircraft, fairly realistic. The fact that, in those days of peace, the task of the 'enemy' was made easier by the relative simplicity of navigating over lighted towns and by the absence of lethal attacks from the ground and air, served to provide a useful exaggeration of the needs of air defence.

Bomber Command had no such opportunities for realistic exercises. Everyone knows that, in the latter half of the war, Bomber Command devastated Germany by night bombing. These operations had to be conducted against blacked-out towns, against intensive opposition from the ground and from the air and against all the wiles the enemy could produce to confuse the approaching bombers. Industrial and artificial smoke, dummy fires, the glare of searchlights and many other artifices made the task of the bombers seemingly impossible. Not only the actual attacks on targets but navigation to them proved at first to be extremely difficult. Radio aids used in pre-war Civil Aviation were in general impracticable in war and astronomical observations, even if cloud conditions permitted them, were not found sufficiently accurate in the hands of the solicitors, bank clerks, commercial travellers and members of a hundred other professions and occupations who had to take them from the unstable platforms formed by their aircraft.

There was no practicable way, in peace, of producing these conditions. While Fighter Command could practise defence over its own ground, flights of hundreds of miles over even a lighted Europe were not, of course, permissible. The difficulties of target-finding might have been disclosed had pre-war exercises been held in which the whole of Great Britain was blacked-out and in which all the conceivable methods of hindering our bombers, short of lethal ones, were simulated. No one can imagine frequent exercises of this kind being held over a pre-war Britain, and in any case few bomber aircraft were available for them.

While still at Worth Matravers, R. J. Dippy, who was entitled to wear the old Bawdsey tie, came to me with an idea, in fact two ideas, though one was to have a greater future than the other. This is one of the incidents of the war which stand out with curious clarity in my mind. I have heard it said that Dippy had put forward these ideas in 1937 but I had heard no mention of them in the intervening years. One idea, known as H, involved the transmission of radio signals over enemy territory which was then not permissible. Times were to change greatly. The other, known as G, and later Gee, aimed at laying down an invisible grid or network of position lines over Western Europe and at providing every bomber aircraft with a special radio set enabling the aircraft's position on this grid to be determined. The radio grid, which covered the Low Countries and the vital Ruhr area, was produced by transmitting accurately timed and synchronized radio pulses from three Gee stations near the east coast. The Gee set in an aircraft enabled the differences between the times of arrival of the pulses from neighbouring Gee stations to be measured and displayed to an observer. Consider for a moment only two coastal transmitting stations, say the centre one and the one to the north of it. If the aircraft Gee set records that the pulses from these two stations arrive at the same instant, it is clear that the aircraft must be equidistant from the two stations and a straight line can be drawn on a map such that every point on it is a possible position for the aircraft, i.e. it is what navigators call a position line. If the pulses from the two stations arrive at different times a position line can still be drawn but it will be curved and there will be a different line for every time difference. If time differences are now measured for two other coastal transmitting stations, another set of position lines will be obtained and the intersection of the two sets of lines constitutes the radio grid. In practice it was found convenient and economical to use only three ground stations. From the centre one and the one to the north of it, a time difference was measured which told the aircraft observer that he was somewhere on a line which he could draw on a map. From the centre transmitting station and the one to the south, another time difference was measured, and this gave another position line on the map. The intersection of the two position lines gave the position of the aircraft.

This navigational system was not strictly a member of the radar family because, although pulses were used, there was no question of reradiation of energy from an object, which is the main characteristic of radar. The great advantages which the system offered for navigation in war were that an unlimited number of aircraft could use it, provided each was fitted with a Gee set; no warning of approach was given to the enemy, and there was no dependence on weather conditions.

Excitement ran high at Swanage at the prospect of extending our activities to Bomber Command. Small-scale tests made in the autumn of 1940 established the practicability of the Gee system, and plans were made for the installation of three high-powered transmitting stations with associated equipment, for laying the Gee grid over Western Germany. Meanwhile, the design of a suitable receiver was embarked upon, and successful flight tests were made with it during the spring of 1941. By July, the ground stations were ready and twelve aircraft were installed with Gee sets and were ready for operational trials by the R.A.F. These occurred in August 1941 and were an outstanding success. It was seen that ability to navigate to the near vicinity of a target in Western Germany was far from being the only service which Gee could render to Bomber Command. Although the Gee grid covered a limited area, knowledge of accurate position at its western fringe enabled bombers to navigate beyond the Gee area with accuracies hitherto unattainable. Not the least of the virtues of Gee was that it enabled tired crews to navigate their aircraft back to their bases without asking aid from the ground and thus breaking radio silence.

The accuracy of a Gee fix depended on the distance of the aircraft from the Gee ground stations. Over Germany it was an aid to navigation rather than to blind bombing, but near home the degree of accuracy was high. During the R.A.F.'s first flush of enthusiasm for Gee we heard the light-hearted story of a pilot of an aircraft approaching its base in bad weather, asking his navigator for steering directions to the aerodrome; the alleged reply was: 'What part of the aerodrome do you want?'

In that summer of 1941, however, there was a grave stumbling-block to the immediate use of Gee over Germany. There were not enough sets. It is commonly supposed that in the 1914–18 war our immediate use of the first few available tanks enabled the enemy to prepare for their use on a larger scale and to start their manufacture for use against us, thus robbing us of much of their value. The timing of the use of a new weapon in relation to the quantity available is particularly important for radio devices because most of them, in time, can be countered by deliberate radio jamming. Bitter arguments on the timing of the use of a new radar device were not infrequent until the war was nearing its end, but, looking back on it all, it is pleasant to record that the right decisions were nearly always taken. Certainly it was right, in the summer of 1941, to await the production of several hundreds of Gee sets before using the device over enemy territory.

We at Swanage were a little unreasonable at this time in our attitude towards delays in production, a problem we did not then understand. One radar device after the other emerged from the laboratories almost without warning and, by some magic, we expected there to be waiting for us a radio industry of the gigantic size which eventually materialized. It is possible, however, that our unreasonableness led to some acceleration of production and to some short-cuts in the long journey from laboratory device to mass production. With regard to Gee, I recall urging (preaching is perhaps a better word) that, because few bomber aircraft could find their targets, one Gee set was equal to twelve bomber aircraft, together with all the heavy expenditure involved in operating these aircraft, and that there should therefore be a vast expansion of production facilities. Some at Swanage felt that if we had the money in our pockets we could collect bits and pieces from radio firms all over the country and get a small firm to make sufficient Gee sets to justify operations against Germany by Christmas. Such was our enthusiasm and eloquence that Sir Frank Smith, Controller of Communications Equipment, obtained agreement to my proposal that £4,000 should be put at my personal disposal for the purchase of components for Gee sets. The money was paid into a Swanage bank, but not a penny of the money was spent. The production of Gee sets was accelerated and the episode of the £4,000 meant no more than that both scientists and production engineers had much to learn from one another.

The story of the operational use of Gee is best told by the R.A.F. Signals and Bomber Command organizations which planned the operations, and by those who used the equipment over Germany. Suffice it here to say that the first Gee raid took place early in March 1942 against a target in the Ruhr. The results showed that a new era in bombing operations had begun. Not least of the merits of Gee was that, by greatly increasing the accuracy of navigation, far more highly concentrated attacks could be made, leading to fewer bomber losses. Soon, in May 1942, the first thousand-bomber raid took place against Cologne; the handling of this number of aircraft in a concentrated attack would have been impossible without Gee. There was no doubt about the warmth of the reception given to Gee by Bomber Command. As one bomber pilot said in a talk to the Swanage scientists: 'We used to be told to bomb Krupps but without Gee we were lost as soon as we left the aerodrome.' There was sufficient truth in the remark for the advent of Gee to be regarded as a turning-point in the story of the bombing of Germany. Let it be remembered however that it was primarily a device for assisting navigation and not a device for the blind bombing of a target.

For me, and perhaps for many others, the joker in the pack of T.R.E. devices was Oboe, though it played the part of an ace. Nearly all of our devices were welcomed by their potential users, not only when trials had established their efficacy but also when they were no more than proposals. Oboe was an exception. When born at Swanage, and when trying to grow, it had few friends outside the Establishment, though Watson-Watt was an exception. There was at least one voice that called for the sacking of the man responsible for 'this fantastic Oboe'. Yet this device was the keystone of the now famous Pathfinder Force of Bomber Command. It was this device which led to the devastation of the Ruhr, described by Sir Archibald Sinclair in the House of Commons as one of the greatest victories in our history. Hitler, when told of the results achieved by the use of Oboe, refused to believe them possible. It might be supposed that, after these successes, the Oboe team would pass into quiet waters, but it was not to be. Until the end of the war I seemed to spend more than a fair proportion of my time trying to calm the Oboe waters, but it continued to be the joker in the pack.

I cannot recall when Reeves, the originator of Oboe, first put forward the scheme. Certainly there was none of the flourishing of trumpets which usually heralded a proposal of major importance. Oboe was a device which, under certain conditions, enabled a bomb to be aimed with a high degree of accuracy in all conditions of visibility, by day or by night. In principle the scheme was simple enough, though the precision aimed at demanded the utmost ingenuity in technique. The scheme involved two ground stations in England, known as the Cat and the Mouse. The Cat station enabled an aircraft carrying special equipment to fly with great accuracy over a target, such as a large factory. The Mouse station calculated the position at which a bomb should be released in order to hit the target and, because the station was able to observe with great accuracy the positions of the aircraft along its path over the target, it was able to send a signal from England telling the crew of the aircraft over Germany when to release the bomb. Surely the critics of Oboe may be forgiven for calling the scheme fantastic! It should be noted that, as with Gee, Oboe is not strictly a member of the radar family because the position of the aircraft was obtained from observations of signals transmitted from it.

Perhaps the obvious limitations of Oboe were responsible for many of the doubts expressed regarding its operational utility. For technical reasons the wavelength for Oboe needed to be short and the $1\frac{1}{2}$ m. region was first chosen. Communication between ground station in England and aircraft over Germany, on this wavelength, necessitated an optical path between the two, and because of the earth's curvature, the aircraft had to fly at a great height. But great flying heights and heavy bomb loads do not go well together and it was clear that Oboe fitted in heavy night bombers could not be used to reach the Ruhr, even though it was less than 300 miles from our shores. Another limitation of Oboe was that the ground stations could only control one aircraft at a time. These limitations gave clear pointers to the need for a Pathfinder Force in Bomber Command and it is puzzling that, following the birth of Oboe, no urge for a Pathfinder Force was immediately forthcoming from any quarter, including Swanage. There was, however, at that time, little contact between Bomber Command and ourselves.

The story of the operational use of Oboe must wait awhile because, before it transformed the operations of Bomber Command against the Ruhr, we had moved elsewhere. But it was at Swanage that Reeves began to collect a few men around him to form an Oboe team, men who bore a great loyalty to him throughout the war. I sometimes think that none but Reeves could have evolved Oboe. Often, on entering his office, I would find him leaning back in his chair with his feet on the table, and a far away look in his eyes; I never ceased to be amused at the time it took him to bring his thoughts back to an awareness that he was not alone. Oboe was born and bred from day-dreams.

In the summer of 1941, we began to hear rumours that all was not well with the bombing of Germany but we found it difficult to get the facts. The day was to come when many Bomber Command officers regarded the Establishment as their second home and when the facts concerning a raid, pleasant and unpleasant, would be known to us within a few hours of the end of an operation. But in mid-1941 no urgent appeals for radar to come to the aid of Bomber Command had reached us at Swanage. In pursuance of my task of showing why radar devices were born at different times, it is well to note that there was good reason for the reticence of Bomber Command. Its bomber crews were attacking Germany under conditions of great difficulty and danger and it was the responsibility of Bomber Command, and not of civilian scientists, to maintain the morale of the crews. The 'ifs' of war are not always a profitable basis for discussion, but there is little doubt that, without the radar devices born at Swanage, the R.A.F. would have been forced to abandon its plans for the devastation of Germany by night bombing. But until such a decision was reached it was important to avoid upsetting the morale of the bomber crews by a disclosure that their efforts were largely wasted.

It was Lindemann, now Lord Cherwell, who, in the autumn of 1941, having obtained the facts about the unsuccessful bombing of Germany, appealed for radar aids for Bomber Command. It is my view that Bomber Command owes much to Lord Cherwell and we at Swanage, and later elsewhere, gained greatly by his powerful support. We did not always agree with his views but throughout the war he proved a stimulating and valuable friend to T.R.E.

When the limelight was thrown upon the work of Bomber Command we took stock of what we had to offer. The nature of Bomber Command's problem was clear. There could be no dependence upon the human eye for locating targets at night and the more aircraft used in a raid the greater the waste of effort. Somehow or other, aircraft had to reach and bomb their targets without relying upon any ground object being seen. Taking stock, it was seen that at least we had made a start. Gee was coming as a navigational device, though its accuracy of position-finding did not suffice for blind bombing. We were working on Oboe but it had limitations and few friends. It was Lord Cherwell in particular who wanted a device with an unlimited range of operation; his eyes were already on Berlin.

Late in October 1941 I held a Sunday Soviet on how to help Bomber Command to bomb unseen targets. Lord Cherwell's insistence on great ranges of operation ruled out systems of the Gee and Oboe types which depended upon ground transmissions from England. We therefore discussed the possibility of self-sufficient equipment in a bomber aircraft which might enable electric power lines to be followed or which might detect towns by virtue of the magnetic field associated with electrical installations. The day ended sadly, for I recall that we went to our homes tired and without an idea. Early in the same week, however, Dee and his team, working on applications of centimetre wavelengths, and Skinner and his team, working on basic problems associated with these wavelengths, discussed the problem further; it was recalled that from 'Centimetre Alley', at Leeson House above Swanage, echoes had been received from the town. There was already little doubt that, with centimetre A.S.V., a map of the sea could be displayed in an aircraft on which any surface vessel within radar range would be shown. There was good reason to suppose that better radar echoes would be got from the smooth walls and roofs of buildings than from the irregular surfaces offered by woods and fields. Why not, then, let a rotating centimetre beam scan the surrounding countryside to produce a picture of towns instead of ships? A centimetre A.I. set at Christchurch aerodrome was quickly modified to provide a beam which could scan the ground area ahead of the aircraft, and on the Saturday following the Sunday Soviet a flight was made to Southampton. Strong indications of the town were seen on the cathode-ray screen. Thus was H_2S born. The code name of H_2S, chosen by Lord Cherwell, was associated

116

with his desire that the equipment should be used for homing on to a target; Home Sweet Home.

Shortly afterwards, flights were made over cloud in which photographs were taken of the screen indications of midland towns. When the still wet prints were laid on my table I am remembered to have said: 'This is the turning-point of the war.' Certainly this was one more of the great moments I recall with curious clarity.

If the then despised Oboe was the joker of the pack of T.R.E. devices, H_2S was the king. Nothing was too good for it. It had, through Lord Cherwell, the personal backing of the Prime Minister who, within a few months of its birth, held a meeting on it which Dee and Lovell attended. Incidentally, our American colleagues were astonished that it was possible for a Prime Minister and working scientists to get round the same table; the Germans would have been still more astonished. The project demanded a major modification of the design of the Halifax and Lancaster night bombers, thus delaying production at a time when aircraft manufacturers were being urged on to greater efforts. Without powerful political support it is doubtful whether H_2S could have withstood the understandable storm of protest which arose at the demands made upon the aircraft firms concerned.

There was, however, a danger that H_2S would suffer from too much limelight and too much haste. Lord Cherwell was calling for the availability of the device by July 1942, seven months after its birth. From Chapter x we have seen what a vast gap exists between a demonstration of laboratory equipment and availability in quantity to the Service user. Recognizing this, Lord Cherwell urged the earliest possible use of the crudest possible equipment. It was his view that, by astronomical methods, navigators should be able to get their aircraft to within a few miles of Berlin and other cities beyond the range of Gee, after which a low-powered H_2S would suffice to home on to the target during the last few miles of approach. He further argued that if semi-developed equipment worked for only the last ten minutes of approach and then broke down, it would have done its job. Lord Cherwell's argument was reinforced by a security factor of great importance. Use of H_2S against Germany inevitably meant making the Germans a present of the results of the revolutionary advances made in centimetre techniques in Great Britain, thus enabling the enemy to copy the device and use it against us. If a homing range of about 10 miles on to a German town were all that was needed, the simplest form of generator of centimetre wavelengths, known as a klystron, could be used and the value of our gift to the German would be minimized. If, however, H_2S were to be used for navigating beyond Gee range by a process of noting the positions of towns throughout the aircraft's flight to its target, a range greatly in excess of 10 miles was needed. To get this range involved disclosing to the Germans radar's most precious secret, the high-powered generator of centimetre wavelengths, the magnetron. We at Swanage did not believe that night bombers could navigate to within 10 miles of Berlin by astronomical observations and we urged the use of the magnetron, arguing that it would take the enemy two years from the date of capture to use H_2S against us on a useful scale. Moreover, we did not believe that a useful device could be evolved of such crudity that only ten minutes of working life was expected of it on each flight. We felt that a set so poorly designed as this was more likely not to work at all!

These conflicting views on H_2S are an example of the discussions which frequently followed the birth of a new device. Service and civilian authorities at Air Ministry and M.A.P., potential users at Commands and the radar

PLATE IV

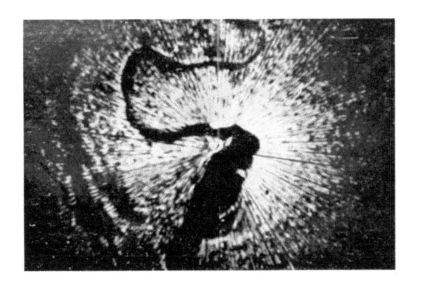

THE RIVER SEVERN
TAKEN BY H₂S MARK III (X BAND),
FROM 1000 FEET

scientists argued, calmly or forcefully after their kind, on what should be done in the best interests of the war. With H_2S a compromise was reached in January 1942 when Lord Cherwell, ever ready to listen to us, agreed to recommend that both the klystron and the magnetron schemes should go forward.

On 1 January 1942, Lovell was given charge of the H_2S project and of the sister project, centimetre A.S.V. His turbulent spirit, high moral courage and boundless enthusiasm contributed greatly to the success of these devices. A few days later a Bomber Command representative, Flight-Lieutenant J. Dickie, visited us at Swanage and flew with the experimental equipment. This was the beginning of an association between Bomber Command and ourselves which was later to become part of our daily lives. Meanwhile, experimental flights continued with an increasing promise of ultimate success. It is not surprising that H_2S lived in a limelight atmosphere, for consider what it offered to Bomber Command. The navigator of a bomber aircraft had before him a screen, like a television screen, on which, whatever the thickness of the clouds below him or the blackness of the night, and however far from home, he could distinguish between large land and water areas as he flew to his target, and could see the shapes of the British coast, of the European mainland and of large estuaries and lakes appear on the screen as the aircraft flew over them. When over land the sensitivity of the device could be reduced so that only large towns appeared on the screen. After the war, the British press described H_2S as 'the magic eye' but there was no magic in the basic principle which enabled an observer to distinguish between water, land and built-up areas. If we stand on a cliff and look out upon a dead calm sea with the sun behind us, the water will look dark because most of the sun's light will be reflected away from us by the mirror-like surface of the sea. If, as we look, a freshening wind disturbs the sea surface, it will look brighter than did the calm sea, because now the sun's light is scattered in all directions from the sea surface and, standing on our cliff, we get a fair share of it. What, however, will look brighter still will be the taut white sail of a boat squarely facing us, because in this case more of the sun's light is reflected back to our position. So with H_2S. When the sweeping centimetre beam from an aircraft strikes water it is largely reflected away from the aircraft and so water is shown as a dark area on the H_2S observer's screen. When the beam strikes ordinary country-side, such as pasture land and wooded areas, the energy in the beam is scattered by the irregular surface and some of it comes back to the aircraft and illuminates that area of the screen which corresponds to the land areas. If, however, the beam strikes a large built-up area, the smooth surfaces of the walls and roofs provide opportunity for multiple reflections, and less energy is lost in general scattering and absorption while more returns to the aircraft. Thus, built-up areas show up clearly against the countryside surrounding them. It sounds simple, but about $\frac{1}{4}$ ton of complicated equipment had to be evolved and installed in every aircraft modified to take it before H_2S could be used for attacking Germany.

As with Oboe, the story of the operational use of H_2S must wait awhile because, before the Germans felt the terrible significance to them of this new weapon, we had moved again.

At the end of our stay in Swanage, few of us doubted that Gee, Oboe and H_2S would eventually enable Bomber Command to devastate Germany. The name of Swanage will surely not be forgotten in the annals of Bomber Command.

CHAPTER XIII

SWANAGE AND FIGHTER COMMAND

WHEN the bulk of the scientific staff left Worth Matravers in the autumn of 1940 and scattered round the Swanage area, Fighter Command still had the first claim on our work and little effort was available for the other potential users of radar. When we left Swanage, in May 1942, research work for Fighter Command occupied a diminishing proportion of T.R.E.'s effort, for radar had provided solutions of day and night defence against aerial attack which largely sufficed for the duration of the war.

The intervening period saw the evolution of A.I. on a wavelength of 10 cm., the dire need for which has already been explained. It is my view that, of all radar devices evolved between 1935 and the end of the war, centimetre A.I. was the most difficult. In Chapter IX we left Dee and his team at Worth Matravers, feeling pleased that, with centimetre equipment on the ground, an echo had been obtained from a Battle aircraft at a range of two miles, but the difficulties which confronted them in their task of evolving an acceptable centimetre A.I. installation in an aircraft might well have daunted lesser men. It is not difficult to see why more was demanded of A.I. than of any other form of radar. No important limitations were imposed on the weight and size of ground radar; heavy bombers and long-range sea reconnaissance aircraft were primarily load carriers and room could usually be found for radar devices. The space available in the fuselage of a twin-engined night fighter was, however, extremely small and every extra pound of weight meant a slower climb to reach an enemy bomber.

To make matters worse, an A.I. set could not be installed just anywhere in a fighter aircraft but demanded the coveted nose position so that search could be made for an enemy ahead. The centimetre beam for H_2S or A.S.V. had only to scan the ground or sea surrounding the aircraft carrying it. Scanning for A.I. involved far greater complications because the target might be above or below and to the left or to the right. Again, A.I. had to provide more accurate angular data than other airborne radar devices and it had to give these data at ranges of a few hundred feet as well as at a range of a few miles.

It is not usually wise to choose the most difficult of all applications for the exploitation of a new technique, but in 1940 Fighter Command came first and an A.I. set was flown in a Blenheim aircraft in March 1941; the beam scanned the sky in front of the aircraft in spiral fashion, the maximum angle to the fore and aft of the aircraft being 45°. On this flight a range of two miles on a target aircraft was obtained with the fighter flying at a medium altitude. This was the first occasion on which an A.I. range was obtained which was greater than the flying height of the aircraft.

The spiral scanner used in these early flights was in itself a remarkable achievement. Its beautiful mechanical design was largely due to Messrs Nash and Thompson, a firm which continued to be invaluable to us throughout the war. Tribute should also be paid to Hodgkin, a member of T.R.E. whose training as a biologist seemed a curious prelude to the outstanding contributions he made to the solution of mechanical and electrical problems associated with centimetre radar in aircraft. It must be confessed that when R.A.F. personnel at Christchurch saw the first A.I. scanner system installed in an aircraft, doubts were cast on the sanity of the scientists. Before the system reached a speed of rotation greater than the eye could follow, it could be watched rotating in a curiously irregular fashion with the one apparent desire of escaping from the aircraft altogether. When however the system was found to do its job and to give less trouble than many devices of greater apparent respectability, the R.A.F. personnel soon learnt to regard it as a normal piece of equipment. One other major problem remained to be solved before centimetre A.I. could become a practicable device, and it is typical of the need and of the spirit of the period that the rest of the work went on without waiting for a solution which might never come. In radio installations, it is customary to use one aerial system for transmission and another for reception and this practice had been applied to airborne radar devices (and to nearly all ground radar sets) prior to centimetre A.I. For the latter device, the tiny aerial was an integral part of the scanning system which, we have noted, made heavy demands upon aircraft space. To fit two such scanning systems, one for transmission and one for reception, was out of the question and somehow or other the one system had to be made to serve both purposes. The G.E.C. Research Laboratories, the Clarendon Laboratory Group and T.R.E. all played their part in finding a solution. By the use of a most ingenious form of switch it was arranged that the same aerial system should alternate with great rapidity between transmission and reception. This success was achieved in May 1941.

Now began a great urge for the production of the new centimetre A.I. equipment and the General Electric Company was asked to make 150 by December 1941. Clearly the ordinary processes of mass production were too slow to meet this demand and so special methods were adopted which made greater demands on highly skilled labour than are usually justified. Meanwhile, the R.A.F. had to be trained by T.R.E. personnel in an entirely new technique and methods had to be evolved for introducing the novel equipment into the R.A.F. It was from this need that the T.R.E. Post-Design Service, described in Chapter x, was born. A separate group was formed under Ratcliffe, which helped to design and construct indispensable test equipment, wrote manuals for the use of R.A.F. personnel and actually fitted the first 36 of the centimetre A.I. sets in aircraft and then lived with the squadrons which used them. The first operational success with the equipment was in April 1942.

To me, the evolution of the first type of centimetre A.I. equipment is one of the grandest stories in the history of radar. In the summer of 1940 there was a cumbersome ground equipment, with its own pumping plant, showing echoes from a man on a bicycle. In less than two years an enemy aircraft had been shot down with the use of centimetre A.I. In this short time, not only had the equipment gone through the research, development and small-scale production stages, but the R.A.F. had been trained to use an entirely novel equipment.

Although anti-aircraft gunnery was not the responsibility of Fighter Command nor research upon it the responsibility of T.R.E., the birth of centimetre radar for directing anti-aircraft fire is a good example of how events in one field can influence progress in other fields. In the autumn of 1940 we at Worth Matravers were feeling it a little hard that although T.R.E. had taken the initiative in applying centimetre radar to the needs of the war, the chosen objective, an A.I. equipment, was the most difficult of all radar applications for any of the three fighting Services. Was there not some way in which we could get quick results? It was, I believe, Lewis who suggested that an attempt should be made to fire an A.A. gun, using centimetre radar, before Christmas 1940. The story of the application of radar to

A.A. gun-fire is for the War Office scientists to describe. Suffice it here to say that A.A. fire directed by radar on wavelengths of from $3\frac{1}{2}$ to $5\frac{1}{2}$ m. was not accurate and that centimetre radar promised far better results.

It was for this reason that, having among the Service Establishments a temporary monopoly of centimetre equipment, we somewhat lightheartedly asked that a nearby A.A. battery and crew should be placed at our disposal and we would do the rest. Wiser counsels prevailed and the War Office team rapidly acquired knowledge of the new centimetre radar techniques. We may however note, as an example of the need for close liaison between defence research Establishments, that it was the T.R.E. work on centimetre radar for A.I. that led directly to the introduction of centimetre equipment into the Navy and Army.

It is not my purpose to describe every radar device evolved by T.R.E., but before leaving the story of the contribution made by radar to the work of Fighter Command it is worth noting the lines on which progress continued to be made. Of these, one of the most important was the application of centimetre radar technique to the Ground Controlled Interception equipment, the $1\frac{1}{2}$ m. version of which has been described in Chapter VIII. With the much narrower beam which the centimetre technique made possible, the positions of bomber and fighter could be plotted with greater accuracy than hitherto and interception therefore made easier. Moreover, radar beacons were provided at R.A.F. Fighter Stations which enabled night fighters, perhaps lost in a chase after a prey, to find their way home with ease. Another service to Fighter Command was the Fighter Direction Station which was a child, albeit a lusty one, of the centimetre G.C.I. equipment. On a Sunday visit to us in the autumn of 1941, Air Marshal Sir Sholto

Douglas, A.O.C.-in-C. of Fighter Command, told us of the troubles he was having with his fighter sweeps over the Pas-de-Calais area and of how important it was to our Russian allies that German fighters should be at least kept busy and wherever possible destroyed. With this object in mind, a Fighter Direction Station was designed and produced which gave the position of aircraft at such great ranges, and with such accuracy, that both hostile and friendly fighters could be watched from a site near the south coast of England, thereby enabling our fighter aircraft to be directed towards those of the enemy. We did not then know that we were taking an important step towards the evolution of devices which later played a vital part in the invasion of Europe.

Mention should also be made of the problem of I.F.F., the identification of friend from foe which, like the poor, was always with us. With the extension of radar to all three fighting Services, equipment on an increasing number of wavelengths became operational and it became increasingly clear during the Swanage era that a separate wavelength would need to be chosen for I.F.F. and arrangements made to provide identification facilities for nearly every type of radar equipment. Much ingenious and difficult work on this problem continued throughout the war.

A story will serve to illustrate the importance as well as the fallibility of identification. Each of two pilots had felt uncertainty regarding the identity of the other and were discussing the incident. One said: 'You were lucky, I was about to open fire,' to which the other replied, 'You were luckier; I did.'

While Fighter Command was being aided by radar to achieve victories at home, by day and by night, the war had spread to the Mediterranean. Although operations in that area were not controlled by Fighter Command, it is convenient at this stage to note that radar followed the spreading of the war. It is known that the Italians could not understand how the few British fighter aircraft based on Malta were always in the air when the Italian bombers arrived; the answer was radar. The Libyan campaign was also greatly aided by radar. The geographical spreading of the war meant that T.R.E. had to provide men to augment the operational research workers already in these areas, men who kept in constant touch with us regarding the use of radar in fields far from Swanage.

CHAPTER XIV

WE LEAVE SWANAGE

I N the early spring of 1942 there was no sign that we were soon to leave Swanage. The bad old days of Dundee seemed long past and facilities for our work were steadily improving. The somewhat small aerodrome at Christchurch had been given up and we had at our disposal at Hurn a well-equipped aerodrome under the command of Group-Captain P. J. King. We had our large model shop at West Howe, plenty of room at Worth Matravers for field experiments and, not least, we had for our centimetre work splendid sites overlooking the town of Swanage and Swanage Bay. It is true that we had no resplendent laboratory buildings, but many of the T.R.E. scientists had a curious preference for working in attics and in odd corners, provided that the necessary electric power facilities were available. Because many of the 1,000 T.R.E. personnel had been recruited from their homes in Swanage, there were no great living and housing problems. Altogether, we were as comfortable as we could expect to be in the middle of a war.

Then came a bombshell, unheralded by rumour. There were, we were told, seventeen train-loads of German parachute troops on the other side of the English Channel preparing to attack T.R.E. The Prime Minister, we were told, had said that we must move away from the south coast before the next full moon. A whole regiment of infantry arrived to protect us; they blocked the road approaches to our key points, they encircled us with barbed wire, they made preparations to put demolition charges in our more secret equipments and, in the execution of their lawful duties, they made our lives a misery. Nor was this all. Our

Home Guard, of considerable strength, was expected to be on duty all night and to work all day. My own time was spent less in dealing with the work of T.R.E. than in discussions on whether we should die to the last scientist or run and, if the latter, where. These events made us co-operate whole-heartedly in the task of finding a place where we could get on with the war in peace.

I do not know whether in fact any German paratroops awaited us across the water and, although I know that the Prime Minister was personally concerned in our move, I do not know whether he ordered our evacuation 'before the next full moon', but I am inclined to doubt both statements. My guess is that our move from Swanage happened in this way. The Air Ministry or M.A.P., or both, began to be worried about our being at Swanage. T.R.E. was passing through an era in which new radar devices were being offered to the R.A.F. at almost disconcerting speed and to bring these devices to fruition meant that the T.R.E. staff was likely to grow rapidly. But, even in 1942, it was realized that the invasion of Europe must come some day and that the south coast would be a probable base of operations. Surely, thought London, we had better move these people before they grow to be immovable. They remembered, too, that minor machine-gun attacks had already been made on Worth Matravers and that worse might come. Continuing my wholly conjectural story, London considered how best to encourage T.R.E. to move gladly. An army unit can be moved by issuing a simple and direct order. London wisely understood that T.R.E. could not be moved in this way. The Establishment was at the top of its inventive form and would have resisted almost anything which involved the waste of a single day. Let us, said London, make their lives so miser-able and their work so impossible, that they will gladly pack all that is theirs and go elsewhere. Hence the story of the

German paratroops, the alleged colourful order, impossible of fulfilment, from the Prime Minister and the regiment of infantry.

It was right that we should move, and we later prospered because of the move; all I need say is that, had London given me the task of encouraging T.R.E. to move gladly, I could not have thought of a better method. Perhaps none of my conjectured machinations happened in London but I like to think they did.

At any rate we at Swanage accepted that a move was inevitable and soon we were poring over maps of England. To find a new home for T.R.E. was not a simple task. We needed laboratories, large and small, with special electric power facilities; space for large drawing offices, workshops and stores, and for the administrative work inevitably associated with an Establishment of 1,000 men and women. We needed open spaces for our experiments and, largely because of the growing importance of our centimetre radar work, we needed an extensive view over the surrounding countryside or over the sea. Moreover, we needed somewhere for the T.R.E. personnel to live. This latter factor is nearly always the greatest difficulty confronting the movement of an experimental Establishment. An army unit is always ready to move and it carries its bedding and kitchen with it. To find homes for 1,000 people in the third year of a war was less simple. Moreover, we needed to allow for growth, although we did not then know that our ultimate strength would be 3,000.

By virtue of their playing grounds, assembly halls, lecture rooms and living accommodation, large schools seemed to offer the most hopeful solution of our problem, though most of them could be dismissed after a glance at the map. Marlborough seemed at first to be a possibility, but after a visit there I had to report that the living accommodation in that delightful little town was totally inadequate and that there was no high ground to provide us with our much-needed view over the surrounding country. An amusing interlude in our search occurred when, under protest, I went down into the bowels of the earth to inspect underground factory space. We would certainly have been safe enough but a place less suitable for radar research could hardly be imagined.

We made little progress toward the selection of a site until B. V. Bowden, one of the stalwarts of T.R.E., said he had heard that Malvern College was empty. An immediate visit was made to Malvern but it was found that, although the College had been evacuated early in the war, it had returned. There was no doubt, however, that Malvern College was a far better site for T.R.E. than was likely to be found elsewhere. What chiefly put it in a class by itself was its position on the side of the Malvern hills, with a view over the Vale of Evesham and part of the Severn valley. There was room enough for laboratories and it was clear that some of the features of the College, such as the assembly hall and the gymnasium, could be put to good, if unusual, uses. Moreover, Malvern was a town of 15,000 inhabitants, large enough, we then supposed, to absorb T.R.E. without great difficulty. In Malvern College, then, we had found an answer to our problem, but could we have it? Suffice it here to say that, because of the Prime Minister's personal concern with our future and because of the splendid attitude of the college authorities to their second evacuation in one war, it was agreed that the Malvern College pupils, then on Easter vacation, would not return. Perhaps this is the moment to say that the dispossessed Headmaster, H. C. A. Gaunt, continued to be our helpful friend throughout the war and to record that, when the war ended, the College returned to its home as soon as was humanly possible.

9-2

There must be thousands of people who, if they remember T.R.E., instinctively think of Malvern. It may surprise some of them to know that I regard the Swanage era as the greatest in the history of T.R.E. It was at Swanage that men of a restless genius formed themselves into teams which worked together with a common purpose. It was at Swanage that radar equipments were born which, in great measure, provided solutions of major war problems and it was at Swanage that we learnt how to contribute to the problem of making new equipments available for operations at the earliest possible moment.

For consider what happened in the two years we spent at Swanage. With the use of G.C.I. and A.I. on a wavelength of about 1½ m., Fighter Command had beaten back the enemy's night bombers and caused them to suffer such losses that, for the remainder of the war, the scale of attack by manned hostile aircraft was unimportant. Bomber Command had been provided with Gee, the first device which made it possible for aircraft to navigate accurately at night over darkened Europe; moreover, Oboe and H_2S had been born at Swanage with results which will presently be told. For Coastal Command there had been an intensification of interest in A.S.V., and the type of A.S.V. with which the Battle of the Bay of Biscay was eventually won was born at Swanage. It was at Swanage that the first attempts were made to apply centimetre radar to the needs of the war and the results obtained were passed on to the Navy and to the Army, who reacted with vigour; this early scientific work on centimetre radar was surely the most revolutionary and far-reaching in effect, in the whole history of radar.

It was at Swanage that many of the best-known features of T.R.E. took shape; the Sunday Soviets, the radar school, the post design services, the trainer group and the model shop. Facilities for experimental flying had grown enormously in our two years' stay in Swanage and we had at our disposal at Hurn the latest types of operational aircraft.

But success in research work depends more on the men who do it, and on how they work together, than on any other factor; the right men will nearly always get the facilities they need. In the spring of 1940 there had collected at Swanage a heterogeneous collection of recruits from England, Scotland and Wales. At times it seemed to me that all they had in common was the intensity of their clamour on what should and should not be done in the interests of the war. In the succeeding two years, one or two found the atmosphere unpalatable and sought useful work elsewhere, but the best remained and a team began to emerge which was unbroken until the war neared its end. In the spring of 1942 the senior men of T.R.E. were no less noisy than they were in 1940, but now there was less of discord and more of harmony in the lively discussions on how best we might do our job and sometimes, it must be admitted, on how others might do theirs.

In the light of later events at Malvern and considering our size, it is curious that T.R.E. left so small a mark on the life of Swanage. The pleasant little town had absorbed us quietly and effectively. The local authorities neither helped nor hindered us and none but the tradesmen seemed to feel either pleasure or regret at our departure.

With the invaluable aid of the Emergency Services Organization of M.A.P. and, once again, the Director of Works at the Air Ministry, intensive preparations for our reception were made at Malvern College. Blocks of cubicles were made into laboratories with benches and special electric power facilities. Offices were fitted with telephones, drawing offices were specially lighted, a workshop was built and the whole area was surrounded by the inevitable barbed wire.

Meanwhile, we at Swanage saw our hundreds of tons of equipment packed into vans which left in a seemingly

133

endless stream for Malvern. On 25 May 1942, the T.R.E. personnel, leaving for the time their wives and children behind them, began to move to Malvern by train and in cars mostly so old that it seemed impossible they could reach their destination. For the last time I made my auto-cycle journey from Swanage to unforgettable Corfe where, at the Old Tea House, I had lived for two years in greater comfort than a man has a right to expect in war.

A week later, Swanage was badly bombed.

CHAPTER XV

EARLY DAYS AT MALVERN

THERE is no doubt that the arrival of T.R.E. was a shock to many who lived at Malvern, for the war had made little impact upon the town. A stray bomb was alleged to have fallen a few miles away but no one quite knew where. There had been no influx of industry, making heavy demands on accommodation. In our innocence we thought that there would be no great difficulty in increasing the population by about seven per cent at a time of great emergency, but we were soon disillusioned. The first problem was to find somewhere for 1,000 men and women to eat and sleep on their arrival. To this end the attractive Winter Gardens at Malvern were taken over as a temporary measure and modified to serve as a canteen. M.A.P. had sent down staff to search for billets and, before we left Swanage, a number of T.R.E. men and women, considered to be specially blessed with charm, had made a house-to-house canvass of most of Malvern. To make matters more difficult from a living point of view, the Air Defence Experimental Establishment, which was the radar Establishment serving the Army, also moved to Malvern at this time. However, on the night of our arrival, all had been fed and all had a roof over their heads, though there were many incidents both grave and gay.

The process of settling down to live in Malvern was influenced by two diametrically opposed attitudes to T.R.E. The average citizen of Malvern clearly did not want us. On the now somewhat crowded buses, the once undisturbed citizens complained that all had been well until we came. Billeting is at best a miserable business but more than usual difficulty was experienced at Malvern. Potential billetors fell ill with alarming regularity and the number of destitute aunts who were being given permanent homes in a few days' time passed all bounds of reason. Some gave shelter on the understanding that billetees were in by ten o'clock at night while others gave it on the understanding that they stayed out, somewhere, until the same hour. There were, of course, many who gladly did everything they could to provide homes for men and women who had been sent to Malvern without any choice in the matter, but it is idle to deny that feeling ran high in the beginning.

Fortunately, there were other influences at work. Never in our travels had we received aid from local authorities, but at Malvern, from the beginning to the end of our stay, the Malvern Council could not do too much for us. The friendly attitude adopted by the Council on our arrival was strengthened later by their meeting with Sir Stafford Cripps, the Minister for Aircraft Production, who, as far as security considerations allowed, told them something of our achievements and of our future tasks. Other local bodies, such as the Women's Voluntary Service, gave their help in full measure at a time when we most needed it.

It is pleasant to record that, as the years went by, we became an integral part of Malvern. There were even grumbles in Malvern that the local newspaper might as well be called 'The T.R.E. Times'. But what we most valued, at the end of the war, were the sincere efforts of the Malvern Council to secure T.R.E. as a permanent Establishment in their town.

In those early days at Malvern there were problems beyond the power of the local Council to solve. The vital need was for homes, not billets. There is no intrinsic reason why scientists in war should be any more comfortable than soldiers, but it is vital to the quality of their work, and therefore to the progress of the war, that they should be as free as possible from all personal worries. The mental strain of their work, continued almost without a rest through the years of war, frequently carried many to breaking-point and some beyond it. Knowing this, I sought approval for a number of hotels and large houses, most of them empty, to be turned into small flats. The Permanent Secretary of the Ministry of Aircraft Production, Sir Archibald Rowlands, obtained Treasury approval for this action. Even this constant friend of ours could hardly have known the extent to which this step enabled the T.R.E. scientists to concentrate upon their vital war tasks. Another innovation at Malvern was the setting up of an R.A.F. Mess in the Abbey Hotel. Owing to the difficulty of recruiting sufficient civilian scientists, the Director of Signals, Air Ministry, had arranged that suitably qualified R.A.F. officers and men should work in our laboratories as though they were civilians. Their number increased so rapidly that an R.A.F. detachment, under Squadron-Leader Truscott, was formed and gave us splendid help for the remainder of the war.

In less than a week of our arrival, work was getting into full swing again. Soon from almost every College window overlooking the Vale of Evesham could be seen the metal mirrors associated with centimetre radar. The junior playing fields, scattered with various ground radar devices, looked like the coming or going of a circus, and the only open space that remained sacrosanct throughout the war was the senior turf on which many famous cricketers had been bred. Soon many of the College buildings were used for unfamiliar purposes; the gymnasium as a large storehouse, the Memorial Library as a drawing office and most of the houses as laboratories, large and small. Yet some of the College buildings more nearly fulfilled their intended purposes. The splendid science building, the Preston Laboratory, was used chiefly for the applications of centimetre radar. Two of the houses were used as hostels and because, for T.R.E., Sunday was an important day of labour, a short service in the lovely College chapel was held each Wednesday morning.

It was however inevitable that temporary buildings should be erected and, by the end of the war, the face of the College was sadly changed, except for the senior turf. The first new buildings to be erected were a workshop and a canteen. Erection of the latter enabled the Malvern citizens once again to use their Winter Gardens and we celebrated the opening of our canteen by an outbreak of food poisoning which gave us undesirable publicity in the press. The outbreak could have happened anywhere but it hardly helped in the task of persuading hundreds of men and women to have three meals each day in the canteen. Fortunately, an empty house had already been taken over as a sick-bay and it came into immediate use.

These events may seem far removed from scientific research for the Royal Air Force, but it is important to remember that an Establishment such as T.R.E. is not merely a collection of laboratories and that its personnel are not all scientists. At no time, even when at the end of the war the civilian and Service strength of T.R.E. was about 3,000, did the scientists and their technical assistants number more than about one-third of the Establishment. The Civil Assistant and Accountant, A. B. Jones, who did as much for T.R.E. as any man, had a large staff whose task it was to provide administrative services for the scientists. Men and women had to be paid, fed, housed and, when sick, given attention which billets could not provide; and they needed vast supplies of stores. The rapid transit of documents from house to house and their safe custody absorbed more staff. Laboratories had to be cleaned and the entrances to the College had to be guarded and the grounds patrolled.

PLATE V

MALVERN COLLEGE FROM THE AIR

Hundreds of draughtsmen and skilled mechanics were needed to support the scientists.

In our early days at Malvern the chores of life were sometimes in danger of robbing us of our visions. It was at this time that I discovered how few shirts per person were owned by hundreds of men at T.R.E. and that laundry facilities were a major factor in maintaining morale. We thought we had solved this problem by a special arrangement which gave us excellent laundry facilities but, alas, the watchful citizens of Malvern caused a question to be asked in the House of Commons.

These examples must suffice to show something of the structure of an applied research Establishment, a structure which bears little relation to the needs of fundamental research workers in a University, and to show that to impose, within a few weeks, a large civilian Establishment on a town such as Malvern is less simple than to move a self-contained Service unit. Fortunately, we were given splendid assistance by M.A.P. Headquarters, not least by Captain Spencer Freeman of the Emergency Services Organization.

While we had been settling into Malvern College the R.A.F. unit at Hurn, known as the Telecommunications Flying Unit (T.F.U.), was no less active in taking over an excellent aerodrome at Defford, about 10 miles from Malvern. This unit continued to grow as T.R.E. grew and at the end of the war its strength in personnel was about 1,600.

It was clear that Malvern College offered us many advantages over sites we had previously occupied, but we sadly missed our model shop at Bournemouth which had barely begun its work when we precipitately left Swanage. As the bulk of our work tended to pass from the early research stage to the design and construction of devices in usable form, so our need for a model shop grew. Moreover, we needed it on our doorstep. In the autumn of 1942 formal approval was obtained for the building of what became known as our Engineering Unit and, a little later, approval was obtained for a hostel to house the men and women it employed. But, in the middle of a war, formal approval was not enough, and we watched with jealous eyes the use of building labour on an American hospital nearby. It was Sir Stafford Cripps who gave us· our Engineering Unit without delays which might well have had serious consequences. When I made a personal appeal to him, he at once saw what the unit could mean to us and to the progress of the war, and he used his great influence to ensure that building labour was provided. A site had been selected in October 1942, but progress was slow until January 1943 when Sir Stafford's intervention took effect. By May 1943 a million bricks had been laid and a floor area of 72,000 sq.ft. was available. Engineering services comprising electricity supply, town gas, process water and steam, compressed air, heating and ventilation, telephones and public address equipment were provided and all was made ready for the installation of machine-shop equipment. The provision of this equipment, valued at more than £100,000, was in itself no mean task. On 1 August 1943 workshop personnel moved into the Engineering Unit which began to provide an indispensable service to T.R.E. scientists and greatly to ease the burden carried by the development and design sections of the radio industry. This Engineering Unit, purposely built outside the confines of Malvern College, was acknowledged, not least by the U.S.A. authorities, to be one of the best of its kind in the world.

It is time to return to the story of the evolution of radar devices at T.R.E. In that summer of 1942 there was plenty of need for our contribution to the war. It is true that the work of Fighter Command continued to prosper; shortly after our arrival, the remains of an enemy night bomber, shot down with the use of G.C.I. and $1\frac{1}{2}$ m. A.I., were scattered nearby. Moreover, we knew that centimetre A.I. was being used in operations. But the affairs of Coastal Command were not prospering and the devastation of Germany by Bomber Command awaited the provision of means for accurate bombing; all that we had at that time to offer was 'jam to-morrow'. Of preparations for the inevitable invasion of Europe there was, to us, no sign.

In the tower of Malvern College there was a beautifully panelled classroom which we had promised not to use as a laboratory. To the west it looked towards the Malvern Hills and to the east over the College grounds and the Vale of Evesham. This was my office until the end of the war and was the scene of many a stormy Sunday Soviet. As in the summer of 1942 I looked eastwards from my window I said, with more pride in T.R.E. than truth: 'This war will be won on the playing fields of Malvern.'

CHAPTER XVI

MALVERN AND BOMBER COMMAND

O F all the radar aids given to the various R.A.F. Commands, those to Bomber Command seem to me the most dramatic. Never, surely, was any Command of the three Services more utterly dependent upon novel scientific devices, and it is perhaps profitable to examine why this was so. Without radar, Fighter Command would still have sent its fighter aircraft by day and night against the enemy. Without radar, Coastal Command would still have sent its forces scouring the seas for submarines. Without radar, these two Commands would certainly have failed in their allotted tasks but, as long as we remained at war, none could reasonably criticize them for using their aircraft as best they could in attempts to fulfil their respective tasks. If a civilian may attempt to judge of these matters, there is to me nothing equally obvious about the decision to invest a large proportion of our industrial and man-power effort in the building up of an enormous night-bombing force. I have no knowledge on the subject but there must have been voices which urged bombing by day when targets could be seen more easily and more often than at night and voices which urged a dozen other ways of using, on land or at sea, in Europe or far afield, the mighty effort absorbed by Bomber Command. There surely is no doubt that the decision to concentrate upon a large night-bombing force was among the half-dozen major factors which led to victory, but the decision was taken when no means for blind bombing were sought or were in sight. This is one of the factors which gives the use of radar in Bomber Command its dramatic value. Of course, if it had been found that our bombing was of little value to the war effort, there could have been a change of policy. But a major change of policy, when industry is geared to a great task, is one of the easiest ways to lose a war.

There are two other factors which, to me, accentuate the drama of the use of radar for Bomber Command. In my view, no other Command had so hard a task in war. The task of marshalling a thousand and more heavy night bombers could only have been achieved by brilliant organization and a great determination which without radar would have been of no avail. Finally, there is the drama of the work of the bombing crews. In the Battle of Britain and in the night interceptions of hostile aircraft, fighter pilots had their glorious hour of adventure, mostly over their home territory. The Coastal Command crews had many long, weary flights for every contact with the enemy. But for sustained misery, courage and endurance, surely the Bomber Command crews must claim prior place. The long hours of flight over hostile territory to the target, the constant perils of A.A. fire and fighter attack, and the long journey home with, all too often, a disabled aircraft, called for the display of sustained heroism without parallel. Perhaps figures mean more than words. If we assume that bomber losses on each flight were five per cent (and they were often more), it is easy to calculate that the chance that a member of a bomber crew will survive twenty flights, alive and free, is only about one in three.

It is for these reasons that those who evolved radar devices for Bomber Command have special reason to be proud that they supplemented the courage shown by those who decided to build a night-bomber force, the administrative skill of Bomber Command in handling their aircraft, and the heroism of the crews. Without radar, through the fault of none, the vast effort spent on Bomber Command would have been perhaps the most wasteful event in our military history.

Oboe continued at Malvern to be the joker in the pack of T.R.E. devices. H_2S had been the subject of the understandable but impracticable suggestion that, in order to avoid even a day's delay, work on it should remain at Swanage. All eyes were on H_2S but few were on Oboe, for the old objections remained. To reach the Ruhr, only the Mosquito aircraft could attain the necessary flying height and it had not the bomb-carrying capacity of the heavy bombers; moreover, one Mosquito aircraft approaching the target needed the undivided attention of the two ground stations in England. There were those who said that the Oboe system would be defeated by enemy jamming after one night of operation and others who said that for a bomber to fly at the constant speed, height and course demanded of the Oboe scheme would be suicidal. But the biggest obstacle to a general enthusiasm for Oboe was that no one, in June 1942, had seen clearly how it could be used to produce large-scale results.

There was however no doubt about the enthusiasm of Reeves, of his right-hand man F. E. Jones and of the small team they built around them. For them, T.R.E. was Oboe and the war was Oboe. It is appropriate at this moment to appreciate the freedom given by Service and civilian authorities at Headquarters to T.R.E. in their development of devices in which trusted members of the staff fervently believed. To see clearly from the beginning how a scientific device, or a war, will ultimately develop, must be a rare event; in my view, it never happens. It follows that it is the duty of Headquarters to support with courage and faith the work of those they have chosen to serve them.

There was no senior man at T.R.E. who did not believe that, somehow or other, the incredible bombing accuracy attainable with Oboe would be turned to practical use. Work therefore went on, not only with a wavelength of $1\frac{1}{2}$ m.

but in the region of the now fashionable wavelength of 10 cm. The latter gave promise of still greater accuracies and of a far greater immunity from enemy jamming.

Progress was so rapid that a decision on how to use Oboe, if at all, could no longer be delayed and the subject was discussed at a Sunday Soviet during the summer of 1942. I recall clearly that all who attended that meeting were agreed that Oboe ought to be used in a Pathfinder Force; more particularly, that Mosquito aircraft carrying Oboe should drop flares on to the chosen target, after which the heavy bombers should bomb the now illuminated target or, if the target were still invisible, should use the flares as aiming points. I do not recall clearly who made the suggestion but I think it likely that credit belongs to members of the Bomber Command Operational Research Section who attended the meeting. Neither do I know whether a Pathfinder Force was in any case in process of formation at this time. We heard, however, that there were powerful voices raised against the formation of a special force to direct the main attack, and there is little doubt that Oboe came as a powerful support to those who thought otherwise.

At any rate, the views expressed at that Sunday Soviet were ventilated in all interested quarters and a decision was taken to use Oboe in a special Pathfinder Force of Mosquito aircraft. Great activity followed. Oboe ground stations were built and calibrated. Mosquito aircraft were installed with the simple equipment needed in these aircraft. The chosen leader of the Pathfinder Force, Wing-Commander (later Air Vice-Marshal) D. C. T. Bennett brought his demonic energy to bear on the practical problems involved in the use of Oboe. The association between Bennett and T.R.E. was to last throughout the war and was one of the most fruitful of our contacts with senior members of the R.A.F. It is not to be supposed that clashes between this

forceful personality and equally forceful personalities at
T.R.E. did not sometimes produce sparks, but our common
way of working and mutual respect produced a satisfactory
basis of co-operation.

Rarely in war is the first use of a device attended with the
brilliant success achieved by Oboe on 21 December 1942.
Hitherto all the efforts of the aircraft firms to produce heavy
bombers, all the brilliant organization of Bomber Command
and all the courage of the bomber crews had failed to
damage Krupp's Works near Essen. But on the night of
21 December it was estimated that 50 per cent of the bombs
fell on the target. This was but a beginning. It is not my
business to deal with operational results; suffice it here to
say that Oboe, first with a 1½ m. wavelength and then with
10 cm., devastated the Ruhr and other areas. It was because
of Oboe that Sir Archibald Sinclair was able, in the House
of Commons, to describe the Battle of the Ruhr as one of the
greatest victories in our history. Moreover, the losses, which
many feared might be high, were negligible as a factor in the
operations; in fact many weeks of Oboe operations were
conducted before a single Mosquito aircraft was lost.

By virtue of its accuracy and method of operation, Oboe
was in some ways the most spectacular of all T.R.E. devices.
Sitting in comfort in England, Oboe operators could follow
with great accuracy the track of a Mosquito aircraft as it
flew over a target 250 miles away and could calculate its
speed. The Mosquito crew had to do little more than obey
simple indications and to release their flares when signalled
to do so from England. There would indeed have been no
difficulty in arranging for the radio signal itself to release the
flares. If a Mosquito aircraft made an unsatisfactory approach to the German target, Oboe operators in England
knew all about it, and so did the Mosquito crew when it
returned.

How far removed was Oboe from our pre-war conceptions of bombing! Surely we had reason to be satisfied with the joker in our pack.

If all was well with the joker, what of H_2S, the king? Here was a device which continued to be the subject of the greatest possible pressure from all responsible quarters and I think it likely that, at this time, no other item of this country's supply programme had an equal priority. Certainly H_2S lacked the great accuracy of Oboe, but its potentialities were clearly greater. Provided the radar production effort was forthcoming, it was seen that every heavy night bomber could be given 'eyes' to detect towns within 30 miles and sometimes more, whatever the conditions of visibility. Moreover, there was no dependence on ground stations in England and the equipment could be used wherever the aircraft could operate. This was a tremendous factor at a time when, we understood, great importance was attached to bombing those industries in the east of Germany which were supporting the attacks against Russia. Moreover, the availability of H_2S meant that no city in the whole of Germany was safe from accurate attack by Bomber Command. Experimental flights made in June 1942 gave excellent results and in the following month Bennett of the Pathfinder Force flew an experimental H_2S set for the first time. Difficult policy decisions, to which reference has already been made, had now to be reached. Should the Pathfinder Force be allowed to use a few H_2S sets for target marking or should the first use of H_2S against Germany await the production of several hundreds of sets? Should the low-powered klystron be used, though it sufficed only for the final run up to a target which had been approached by other means, or should we make Germany a present of our precious magnetron by using H_2S for navigation as well as for blind

10-2

bombing? Long and furious were the debates on these subjects. T.R.E. favoured the use of the magnetron as soon as sufficient sets were available to serve the needs of the Pathfinder Force. We argued, and we were not alone, that navigators of bomber aircraft needed all the aid they could get; that Germany would need at least two years to produce a form of H_2S; that strategic bombing was more practicable for us than for an enemy already committed to the enormous industrial demands of the Eastern Front; and that, because of relative distances from aerodromes to targets, navigation was more important to us than to the Germans and that to give the enemy even the klystron would enable him to use blind bombing against London. That civilian scientists at T.R.E. took an active part in discussions of this kind was a vital factor in the co-operation between Service user and civilian scientists. I do not recall a single dictatorial order being given on matters of this kind. Somehow or other, after heated discussions, the right course to take became clear to all, or nearly all.

In July 1942 it was decided that a crash programme should be undertaken by Industry for the production of H_2S sets in numbers sufficient for the Pathfinder Force and that production in the greater numbers needed for the main bombing force should follow by more normal methods. We had had crash programmes before but never one like this. A 'crash' programme implied that instead of undertaking the normal process of tooling for production so that the minimum of highly skilled labour was used, sets should be almost hand-made, whatever the demands on skilled men. The same process had to be applied to the major modifications of the bomber aircraft needed to provide room for the H_2S equipment. A crash programme meant also that the design of the equipment was influenced more by the need for rapid production than by the attainment of the best performance.

High-level interest in a scientific device at an early stage is not always conducive to speed of evolution but there is no doubt that the use of H_2S against the enemy was greatly accelerated by the personal interest of the Prime Minister and Lord Cherwell in the device. The Prime Minister's meeting, already referred to, was held in July 1942 and from then onwards no effort was spared to provide Bomber Command with H_2S. The firm chosen to do the detailed design work prior to production was the Electrical and Musical Industries Ltd. (E.M.I.) and it was decided that the first production orders should be given to the Gramophone Company. For the former, the decision meant an early and deplorable tragedy: at an early stage, the splendid E.M.I. team of research engineers was shattered by the death, in an experimental flight with H_2S, of three of its most senior members; the R.A.F. crew and a T.R.E. scientist, to whom the country also owed much, lost their lives in this accident.

Meanwhile, the whole process of preparing for the use of a new radar device went on apace. Test equipment was made, training devices were evolved and R.A.F. personnel were taught how to use and maintain the equipment. By February 1943 all was ready and Hamburg was chosen for the first target. For Germany, the devastation of Hamburg was a sign of the wrath to come and for Bomber Command it was yet another revolution in bombing, rendered possible by radar.

The devastation caused in Germany by Bomber Command is known throughout the world. For targets beyond the Ruhr, the vast scale of this devastation dated from the use of H_2S. Of course, neither H_2S nor Bomber Command's use of it was at once perfect. In particular the very size of Berlin caused difficulties and a modified form of H_2S equipment was evolved to deal more effectively with the German capital. The so-called Battle of Berlin began in November 1943; it had awaited a few modified H_2S sets prepared in our Engineering Unit and installed in Pathfinder Force aircraft at T.F.U., Defford. So close were we to the war.

If I decline to deal with operational results, it must not be supposed that we had no knowledge of them. On the contrary, within a few hours of an operation over Germany, members of Bomber Command had told us all that was known of the results of a raid on the previous night. Those were tremendous days. The intimacy between some of the senior staff of Bomber Command and the T.R.E. scientists reached a level hitherto unapproached; an intimacy which, curiously enough, far exceeded that between T.R.E. and their scientific colleagues in the Operational Research Section of Bomber Command. Detailed bomb plots, as far as they were known, were later sent to us by our R.A.F. associates and photographs of the devastation were displayed for the encouragement of all at T.R.E. who had helped to achieve these awful results.

We knew that the bombing of Germany was horrible but we knew also that it was indispensable to victory and that it would vastly reduce the losses of the allied armies when the day came to invade Europe. We knew, too, that a few hundreds of one radar device, H_2S, had vastly increased the efficacy of bombing and had ensured that the brilliant organization of Bomber Command and the awe-inspiring courage and endurance of its air crews were not in vain.

The main task of Bomber Command was to conduct a strategic and systematic bombing of Germany's industrial targets, month after month and year after year, until Germany was unable to produce enough of the tools of war to avert defeat. Success in this long drawn-out process depended upon keeping the average loss rate at a tolerable figure. As Tizard pointed out, to halve bomber losses over a long period of strategical bombing is equivalent to a doubling of bomber production. If it is vital to the progress of the war that one particular target, such as a battleship, be destroyed at all costs, a loss rate of 100 per cent can be accepted provided that the bombers' task is properly done; but for strategical bombing through the years, the average loss rate must be small enough to enable attack to be sustained. In their night-bomber effort against us in the early part of 1941, the German losses sometimes reached 10 per cent and we know that the attacks were discontinued as a strategic policy.

To us at Malvern, one of the great puzzles of the war was why Germany allowed Bomber Command to achieve its results. To reach London the German night bombers had to fly only 100 miles or so from aerodromes in France and in the Low Countries, while our bombers had to fly 600 miles to reach Berlin. For us, only a short interval of time was available for the operation of locating devices and for interception by night fighters, while it seemed to us that the Germans had all the time in the world. We used to say, with some truth as well as egotism, that if T.R.E. were in Germany the work of Bomber Command would be impossible. What is more nearly true is that if the Service user and the radar scientist had got together in Germany as they did in this country, the war might well have taken a different course and would certainly have cost us more dearly.

Many factors were responsible for keeping our losses at a level which, though sad, was acceptable in the awful business of war. Selection of the bomber routes best calculated to avoid enemy defences, feint attacks and other artifices must have called for brilliant organization at Bomber Command, but these methods of avoiding losses would have been difficult without radar navigational aids, such as Gee and H_2S. Another vital factor in reducing losses was the high concentrations of aircraft used by

Bomber Command, in itself a great feat of organization, made possible by Gee. In Chapter VIII I have described the combined use of the Ground Control Interception set (G.C.I.) and Air Interception (A.I.) equipments against hostile bombers which came over in an attenuated stream. The Germans also developed a form of G.C.I. and it was so much more accurate (and more cumbersome) than our own $1\frac{1}{2}$ m. equipment that they apparently felt that A.I., the most difficult of all forms of radar to instal in aircraft, was unnecessary. If, however, the sky is full of aircraft passing over a G.C.I. system the operators can only concentrate on one or two at a time, leaving the others unmolested. The Germans also concentrated on the use of radar for illuminating our bombing aircraft by searchlight; this greatly aided A.A. gun-fire, which they did not stint, but searchlights demand clear nights. Radar enabled aircraft to navigate and to bomb while above cloud, thus, in cloudy conditions, defeating the enemy's searchlight system.

A full description of the role of radio and radar in keeping bomber losses to an acceptable level does not fit conveniently into the pattern of this book, but work on this problem occupied one of the liveliest Groups at T.R.E. from 1942 until the end of the war. It was while we were at Swanage that Cockburn, who had not long since joined us from the Royal Aircraft Establishment at Farnborough, paced up and down my office describing in dismal terms what would happen if we did not start research on the problems involved in conducting a radio war; a war in which we should seek to protect our own radio devices from interference while denying full use of radio to the enemy. I suggested that he should go and do something about it and so a special group was formed which was one of the most successful, as well as one of the noisiest, at T.R.E. The noise was not made less by the attachment to T.R.E. of Wing-Commander

Derek Jackson for work in connection with the now well-known Window; this was the code name for the strips of metallized paper which confused the enemy's radar systems. We had met Jackson in 1942 in connection with our devices for use against night bombers; as a scientist he understood what we sought to do and as an observer in a night fighter he contributed to the loss of many a German aircraft. We were indeed glad to have him with us at Malvern, though his presence did nothing to provide an atmosphere of peace and calm at an already somewhat emotional Establishment. A ditty I was one day to write for a farewell party to the American scientists had Derek Jackson as its theme but it would have been applicable to many of the best of the T.R.E. scientists:

> There's peace and quiet where Boffins meet
> Till enters Derek Jackson,
> Who raves and roars and stamps his feet,
> Should not his name be Klaxon?

The work of minimizing bomber losses provides one other example of the birth of a large and important R.A.F. organization arising from the recommendation of a civilian research Establishment. It was T.R.E. who recommended the formation of R.A.F. 100 Group which did so much to defeat Germany's defensive measures.

CHAPTER XVII

MALVERN AND COASTAL COMMAND

A T the time of our leaving Swanage the position of the battle against the enemy submarines was gloomy. The Bay of Biscay ports were in full use and although Coastal Command aircraft, fitted with $1\frac{1}{2}$ m. A.S.V., had achieved a number of successes since as early as February 1941, the shipping losses were increasing with the enemy's submarine strength. Submarines were mostly surfacing at night and, although they were not infrequently located, the difficulty of attacking them except in full moonlight had not been overcome. Hope for the future lay in centimetre A.S.V., but this device had to take second place to its sister equipment H_2S; moreover, even with centimetre A.S.V., the problem of delivering a lethal attack remained unsolved.

I have sought to show that, without this or that radar device, the R.A.F. would have been unable to fulfil its most vital tasks, thus inferring that these devices were indispensable to success. We shall presently see that success against enemy submarines at night depended upon a device which did not involve radar and which did not emanate from T.R.E. To most of us, indispensability is an unpalatable word but this is perhaps the moment for me to describe the sense in which it may fairly be used in connection with an item of scientific equipment.

If a Service department, such as the Air Ministry, proposes to build up a force for the night bombing of Germany, or for preserving our merchant shipping in the face of submarine attacks, it no doubt takes stock of the resources likely to be at its disposal. We can imagine it deciding that, in our highly industrialized country, the aircraft and engines can be built; that the intricate instruments which are needed before the aircraft can perform their tasks will be forthcoming and that armament equipment in the form of bombs, depth charges and guns can be made. We can also imagine the department deciding that man-power suffices for the vast business of maintaining the aircraft and their complicated equipment and that there will be men of skill and courage who will fly them. Any one of these items and a hundred others, including the supply of engine fuel, can logically be described as indispensable because, without it, there would be no bombing or submarine-hunting force. If, when the force has been built up and used in operations, it is found that it is greatly inferior to its task, many things may happen and we can usefully consider three of them. First, it may be decided to renounce the aim for which the force was set up, e.g. it may be decided not to operate night bombers against Germany or not to use the R.A.F. to protect our merchant shipping. Secondly, it may be decided that the force must be multiplied many times if it is to perform its task; if this means a multiplication factor of ten, the country's efforts will be strained to the utmost and other war plans, such as invasion by land forces, may have to be given up. Thirdly, some new scientific device, unconceived at the time of the original planning, may emerge to render the force far more effective.

It is to devices of this kind that a qualified indispensability may be attributed. It is certainly true that, without radar, the tasks of hitting German targets at night or of locating submarines would have involved forces beyond our resources. That the original planning was done without knowledge that unforeseen scientific devices would be essential to success is not a criticism of the planners, for the alternative is usually to do nothing and thus to make defeat certain. At the same time it is important to note that, as a result of our war experiences, scientists are now brought into the initial planning stages.

The device which made lethal attack on a submarine at night possible may claim the kind of indispensability to which reference has been made. This device, known as the Leigh Light, was a powerful searchlight mounted in a retractable cupola beneath the fuselage of the Wellington aircraft, which could, within limits, be directed to illuminate a submarine target. Because the Leigh Light was not a radar device, we were spared knowledge of what the long-suffering aircraft manufacturers thought of this new burden laid upon them. We at T.R.E., however, were not less delighted than Coastal Command at the success of the Leigh Light, for without it A.S.V. sufficed chiefly to frighten submarines at night and rarely to destroy them.

In June 1942 the Leigh Light was fitted to Wellington aircraft carrying $1\frac{1}{2}$ m. A.S.V. Radar sufficed to enable aircraft to home on to a submarine; switching on the Leigh Light when the target was about one mile ahead sufficed to provide something like daylight conditions for the attack. At best, the life of a submarine crew in war is a nerve-racking business. Owing to the submarine's own noise an aircraft cannot be heard approaching; at night it can rarely be seen and by day approach from above clouds or from the sun's position makes detection difficult. In addition, there is the constant menace of the Royal Navy. Before the advent of the Leigh Light, submarine crews proceeding on the surface at night to charge their batteries could regard themselves as tolerably safe from lethal attacks. It therefore needs little imagination to understand that the constant possibility of being suddenly immersed in a flood of light from an attacking aircraft was a further strain on the morale of U-boat crews. During the months of June and July, in spite of losses, the U-boats in the

Bay of Biscay area continued to surface at night, but in August 1942 they had been driven to the desperate remedy of charging their batteries in daylight. Presumably it was felt that they then had a better chance of seeing approaching aircraft before attacks could be made upon them. This change of plan gave Coastal Command its opportunity and in September 1942 nearly forty submarine sightings occurred during daylight hours.

All concerned knew what the Germans should do to swing the battle once more in their favour. What was happening was no mystery to the German Navy, for at least one set of 1½ m. A.S.V. was in their hands. All that was necessary was for every U-boat to be fitted with a radio listening device which would receive energy from the wide beam inseparable from 1½ m. A.S.V. and would provide a visual or aural signal indicating that a radar-fitted aircraft was in the vicinity. The U-boat could then dive to safety, for radar was useless against a submerged submarine. Doubtless the Germans lost little time in fitting their submarines with listening devices but, to us, it was precious time. The Germans had their troubles; submarines had to be fitted with the new device as and when they returned from operations and operators had to be trained to use the equipment. Moreover, it is not to be doubted that some U-boat Commanders regarded a telescope as superior to any new device inflicted upon them. So it came about that in the summer of 1942 we gained time in what was surely the most crucial of all battles of the war, the battle to keep the seas open for the allied merchant fleets.

But by the early winter it was clear that listening for our radar signals was in general operation. Few submarines were sighted and once again shipping losses took an upward turn which had at all costs to be stopped if the war were to be won.

If the Germans knew the answer to our $1\frac{1}{2}$ m. A.S.V., we in this country knew that the answer to their listening devices installed on submarines was the use of 10 cm. A.S.V. Moreover, the range of location of a submarine by $1\frac{1}{2}$ m. A.S.V. was only about four miles, while the range provided by centimetre A.S.V. was several times this value. Not only, then, would centimetre A.S.V. defeat the U-boat's $1\frac{1}{2}$ m. listening device but it would vastly increase the area which could be searched for submarines during the period of an aircraft's patrol. Further, the practice of listening and diving was more difficult for the enemy to put into effect against centimetre A.S.V. than against the earlier type. A continuous signal from our $1\frac{1}{2}$ m. A.S.V. told the U-boat commander with fair certainty that he was in the broad radar beam radiated ahead of an approaching aircraft. With centimetre A.S.V., indications would be received by the listening device whenever the continuously rotating beam swept through the U-boat's position, whether or not the aircraft was approaching the U-boat. Of course, still more complicated devices could have been used by the enemy to give some indication of the degree of danger to a particular submarine, but they would have been far from infallible. A possibility open to a U-boat commander would be to dive whenever there was the slightest sign of danger but his vessel would then be of little offensive value and his crew would soon be nervous wrecks.

Altogether, in that autumn of 1942, we were most sanguine about the ultimate defeat of the U-boat by aircraft fitted with centimetre A.S.V., particularly since the number of aircraft needed for the Bay of Biscay patrol was very small in comparison with the air armada needed by Bomber Command. Why, then, was there any delay in providing and installing the few centimetre A.S.V. sets needed for the task? There were two causes of a little delay.

First, there was the question of priority. The H_2S and the centimetre A.S.V. sets were similar in design; the same scientific staff supervised the two sets which, indeed, were so nearly one that the whole project was called $H_2S/A.S.V.S.$ the final S. denoting the use of short waves. The highest priority was given to H_2S for Bomber Command and centimetre A.S.V. had to wait. This was one of the very few priority decisions with which I personally disagreed, largely because I feared that use of the obvious remedy for our shipping losses would be indefinitely delayed. The second cause for delay involved the old story of the use of the magnetron. It was rightly undesirable to risk disclosure of the magnetron through the capture of centimetre A.S.V. before this precious secret was in any case disclosed by the inevitable loss of an H_2S set during a bombing operation.

However, a decision was made in the autumn of 1942 to divert a number of H_2S sets for use as A.S.V.S. in Wellington aircraft fitted with Leigh Lights. On 1 March 1943 two Wellington aircraft so fitted undertook the first patrol of the Bay of Biscay with centimetre A.S.V.; one of them carried a member of the T.R.E. staff who had helped, as part of our Post-Design Services, to get the equipment installed and operated.

Now came one of those series of tremendous events which sent a thrill through every member of T.R.E. concerned in them, and which did so much to hearten a tiring staff to further efforts. It all happened so quickly. During the late spring and summer of 1943 our Coastal Command friends kept us in touch with results which, with increasing certainty from week to week, meant victory over the U-boat, a victory as decisive as any in the war.

After the Germans had countered our $1\frac{1}{2}$ m. A.S.V. the U-boats had turned to their favoured practice of surfacing at night. In April, with the advent of centimetre A.S.V., they were again forced to surface in daylight and the growing forces of Coastal Command, using new lethal weapons, took heavy toll of the U-boats. In May 1943 nearly one hundred sightings of submarines by aircraft occurred and it was calculated that, on the average, every U-boat operating in the Bay area was sighted twice. Realizing that it was facing disaster, the German U-boat Service even resorted to moving through the Bay area in threes and fours, remaining on the surface in daylight to fight the attacking aircraft. Aircraft were lost, but the more costly submarines were sunk in greater numbers than ever before. Meanwhile the British Navy, with the aid of radar, was also making its great contribution to the defeat of the U-boat. Many will recall announcements at this time, by the Prime Minister and others, of three submarines sunk in one day and of more submarines than merchant ships sunk in one month. From June 1943 our merchant shipping losses were negligible as a factor in the outcome of the war. This was the virtual end of the German U-boat Service and many, on both sides of the Atlantic, who were concerned with the coming invasion of Europe must have felt that a heavy load had been lifted from them.

In the late summer of 1943 Hitler announced on the radio that 'the temporary setback to our U-boats is due to one single technical invention of our enemies'. It is but fair to Hitler to say that he had some reason to believe that the setback was temporary. Already, in Germany, technical men saw how radar could be largely defeated as an anti-submarine device. They must have reasoned somewhat in this fashion. Radar is useless when our submarines are submerged, so need they ever come to the surface, even to charge their batteries? As a result of reasoning such as this the Germans developed Schnörkel, which enabled submarines to remain almost wholly submerged at all times.

In a story of radar we need only note that exhaust gases were taken up through a large vertical exhaust pipe, several feet of which remained above the sea surface. It is one thing to detect a modern surfaced submarine by radar and quite another to detect a few feet of exhaust piping. At a sacrifice of speed, Schnörkel greatly reduced the range of location of a submarine by visual means or by radar and greatly increased the difficulty of delivering a lethal attack upon it.

But the Germans were too late. Schnörkel, like every technical device in war, needed time to produce, time to fit and time to train crews in its use. When it appeared, our armies were advancing fast across Europe and the end was in sight.

In our Sunday Soviets and other meetings at T.R.E. we used often to talk of 'buying time' and the defeat of the U-boats serves to illustrate what we meant. In theory, nearly all radar devices could in time have been defeated by the enemy, provided that sufficient effort was put into countering them. Sometimes voices were raised against the initiation of work on a radar device on the grounds that the enemy would counter it by jamming or by other means. Fortunately, the majority of those concerned, both Service and civilian, were not prepared to adopt this defeatist attitude. The cardinal question was not whether the enemy would one day render a radar device useless, but how long it would take him and what effort he would need to do it. In other words, how much time would a radar device enable us to buy?

With the anti-submarine campaign we have seen that both the $1\frac{1}{2}$ m. A.S.V. and the centimetre A.S.V. equipments were defeated by the enemy, and we have seen the nature of the battle of wits between the opposing sides. Success with $1\frac{1}{2}$ m. A.S.V. was achieved as early as February

1941 but, until the advent of the Leigh Light, it was insufficient to force the enemy to alter his methods or to evolve and instal new equipment. The combined use of the Leigh Light and $1\frac{1}{2}$ m. A.S.V. reduced our shipping losses for several months, caused considerable casualties to the U-boat fleet and made the enemy alter his plans of operation. In our Sunday Soviet jargon, time had been bought. The use of centimetre A.S.V. is a still more striking example. What influenced the outcome of the war was not that a radar device introduced in March 1943 was defeated some two years later but that, in the interval, the submarine had been defeated and the seas made virtually free for our merchant shipping.

I have introduced this matter because of its great importance. There are plenty of reasons why, for example, a new radar device should not be fitted to an aircraft. Aircraft coming from the production line will be delayed by modifications to them, added weight will reduce bomb or fuel load, a further development and production load will be added to the particular Industry which has to make the device, more man-power is absorbed in maintaining the new equipment and more time spent in training personnel to use it. If, in addition to these objections to any new device, powerful voices contend that it is possible for the enemy to counter the device, it may well be stillborn. We in this country owe a great debt to the leaders of the Royal Air Force who brought faith and hope to the process of buying time.

No account of the defeat of the U-boat menace would be complete without reference to the close, informal co-operation between Coastal Command and T.R.E. Co-operation occurred at all levels, but the attitude to T.R.E. of the two successive Air Officers Commanding-in-Chief of Coastal

Command who held office during the most active periods of the war against the submarine, is worthy of note. This is especially so because although Commanders-in-Chief, like Heads of Experimental Establishments, are no more than members of a team, there is a tendency for staffs to follow their lead in relationships with other bodies. During the first period of the U-boat war with which T.R.E. was intimately concerned, the Commander-in-Chief at Coastal Command was Air Chief-Marshal Sir Philip Joubert. Joubert's attitude to scientists was not born of contact with T.R.E. for as early as the late 1920's he sought direct contact with working scientists in his efforts to provide something new and something different for the R.A.F. To us at T.R.E. he was ever a source of inspiration and encouragement on the occasion of his frequent visits. His successor, Air Chief-Marshal Sir John Slessor, was a newer friend, but no less a friend. I remember seeing this Commander-in-Chief of Coastal Command, at the time of a bitter struggle with the U-boats, standing with his coat off in a laboratory building composing with A.S.V. scientists a policy letter to the Air Ministry. We may indeed be glad that this incident could not have happened in Germany. If it is true, as I think it is, that the R.A.F. was saved by radar from frustration and defeat, no Service more deserved the help that came to them from close co-operation with the scientists.

CHAPTER XVIII

MALVERN AND THE INVASION
OF EUROPE

L IKE every corner of the land, T.R.E. was not lacking in amateur strategists. We did not of course always agree among ourselves on how to avoid losing the war and, later, on how to win it, but we seemed curiously unanimous about the invasion of Europe. Before reaching Malvern there had been occasional discussions on how radar might help in this mighty task, but until the autumn of 1942 it was difficult for most of us to think seriously of great armies marching into Germany. At this time there came a number of stupendous world events which turned the tide of the war on land: El Alamein, the landing of the allied armies in north Africa, the encirclement of the German 6th Army before Stalingrad and the decisive battle of Guadalcanal; all within four mighty weeks.

It was at last possible to think of the invasion of Europe as an event which would one day happen. Although we did not sink to the depths of ignorance displayed by those who called, with chalk upon the wall, for a 'Second Front Now', we felt entitled to consider how radar might best be used when the day came. My own view was that, until the submarine had been defeated, there could be no successful invasion of Europe.

I have tried to show that at T.R.E. we did not experience that fierce and automatic opposition which Service chiefs are supposed to display on being presented with new ideas. On the contrary, the R.A.F. welcomed new ideas and were hungry for more. Not only were nearly all our proposals for

PLATE VI

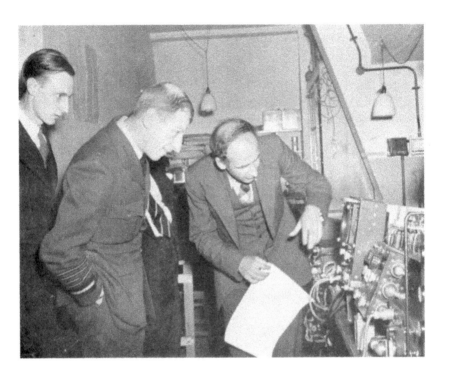

IN A T.R.E. LABORATORY

Dr F. C. THOMPSON   Dr A. C. B. LOVELL
LORD PORTAL (C.A.S.)

new devices given full consideration but our views on the tactics and strategy of their use were given a hearing and often accepted. If I said that there were no exceptions to this happy state, my sincerity might be open to doubt. I have already referred to Oboe as an example of a device which, in the early stages, had few friends outside T.R.E. The only other major matter on which we found difficulty in getting a hearing was the subject of invasion. Looking back on it all, it is good to find that there are in most cases simple explanations of the frustrations we sometimes felt. Even by the end of 1942 our informal relations with the R.A.F. authorities at Headquarters and at Commands were very close, and if invasion had been wholly a matter for the R.A.F. it is not to be doubted that full and free discussions on radar aids to invasion would have been held. Invasion was, however, a matter for the three Services and it was too much to expect that the other two Services would completely understand the nature of our informal contacts with senior R.A.F. personnel, which involved discussions of a nature and scale perhaps hitherto unknown between Service user and laboratory scientist. As one Army colonel said to another after his first visit to T.R.E.: 'That's a funny place. They won't touch a soldering iron unless you tell them all the plans for the campaign in Libya.'

Having by now acquired a faith that at the end of a Sunday Soviet something like the best action to take would begin to appear, we held a meeting solely on the subject of radar aids to invasion. It was a failure. I recall little of that meeting except that, after hearing a description of radar devices which might be used, a visitor said: 'Why do we want all this? We had nothing like it in Crete'!

In spite of a lack of encouragement we did not then understand, we formed an Invasion Panel to consider how radar might some day aid the invasion of Europe. There was a fine-sounding, if somewhat pretentious, ring about the name of this panel, which was started late in 1942; already invasion seemed a little nearer. The senior members of T.R.E. most concerned with these discussions were Lewis, R. A. Smith and J. W. S. Pringle and they found plenty to discuss.

Some of the radar aids used for the invasion of Europe will be described, for the sake of tidiness, in the chronological order of their use on that operation. In selecting examples of successful radar aids, I must plead guilty to displaying wisdom after the event. Moreover, it should be understood that I am describing only the contributions made by T.R.E. Radar Establishments serving the Navy and the Army also made their contributions.

Chronologically, the first step in preparing for the invasion of northern France was the destruction by air bombing of as much of the enemy's resources for resisting the invasion as the allied air power permitted. Of course, the British and American strategical bombing of German industries had already reduced Germany's power to resist invasion. Without the use of radar in Bomber Command and in the American 8th Air Force, the number of tanks, aircraft and other items of war equipment available to Germany on D-Day would have been immensely greater. As part of the final preparations for D-Day, however, there remained the task of bombing targets of special and immediate use to the enemy in his attempts to resist invasion. Obvious targets were enemy aerodromes in France and in the Low Countries, bridges and centres of rail communication, the destruction of which would hinder the movement of enemy troops, coastal batteries and radar installations. Both Bomber Command and the Tactical Air Force contributed to the British effort directed to the destruction of these and other targets. Bomber Command had by this time come to rely on radar for the efficacy of its night bombing but, during a period of excellent weather in the spring of 1944, both Bomber Command and the Tactical Air Force achieved splendid results by day without the use of radar. As had been visualized by the T.R.E. Invasion Panel, however, great use was also made of Oboe and of H, particularly at night against railway centres and marshalling yards, H has been mentioned in Chapter XII as having been proposed simultaneously with Gee. It was a system which gave considerable accuracy of blind bombing by enabling position to be determined from a measurement of ranges from two ground stations. In practice it was found convenient to make the same set perform both Gee and H functions and it therefore became known as G/H. In order to withhold from the enemy a knowledge of the intended landing points, it was necessary to leave the destruction of some targets until the last possible moment. Some of us at T.R.E. had been told of the importance of destroying, a few hours before the landings, the coastal batteries which it was feared might cause heavy losses to our transports. I think there were eleven of these batteries. None in any way concerned will however forget the appalling weather experienced in the days preceding and following 6 June 1944. It was under these conditions that Oboe achieved one of the most spectacular successes of the invasion. On the night preceding D-Day, Oboe was used by Bomber Command to mark the position of these batteries and, as a result of the subsequent bombing, not one of the batteries fired a shot against the D-Day armada. When, on a windy night of thick cloud, the crews of the coastal batteries found themselves subjected to accurate bombing, they may well have felt that they were fighting a race of magicians. That night was another score for Oboe, the joker of the T.R.E. pack.

Chronologically, the next contribution made by T.R.E. devices to the invasion of Europe was the navigational assistance given by Gee to the vast armada of large and small craft which, in bad weather, by day and by night, crossed the English Channel to the beaches of Normandy. For the small distances of the ships from the southern coast of England, Gee sufficed to give positional data with an accuracy unobtainable by any other available means. This is not the place to enlarge upon the magnitude of the task of installing Gee on ships and of training ships' personnel to use the device since, except at the beginning, the work was not the responsibility of T.R.E. but of an Admiralty Experimental Establishment. There is however no doubt about the magnitude of the contribution which Gee made to the success of the initial landings in Europe. Indeed, one grateful Naval officer said that 6 June 1944 should be called Gee-Day rather than D-Day.

When the T.R.E. Invasion Panel began its work in 1942 it was not surprising that one of the first problems which engaged its attention was how best to aid paratroops to land at predetermined points. Both the Germans and the Soviet troops had used airborne forces on a large scale and few doubted that we should some day need to do the same. The essence of the problem is the accuracy of the drop; landing on one bank of a river may mean success, while landing on the other bank may involve disaster. The problem is further complicated if paratroops have been dropped at an unintended point; it may then be better to reinforce them by further drops at that point rather than to correct the error and so scatter the airborne forces. From considerations of this kind were born two T.R.E. equipments known as Eureka and Rebecca. Eureka was a radio beacon carried by the first airborne force to be dropped in a particular area. In principle, the beacon was operated when the force was satisfied that it was in the intended position and was ready for reinforcements. The beacon emitted pulsed radio signals which were received by Rebecca, a device carried in the troop-carrying aircraft used to reinforce the first troops to be dropped. Rebecca enabled the troop-carrying aircraft to home on to the beacon and gave the distance of the aircraft from the beacon. It is to be noted that Eureka and Rebecca, like Gee and Oboe, were not true radar devices, since direct and not reradiated signals were used for the determination of position. These devices had a difficult birth and early experiments with them were somewhat clandestine in character. Although formal recognition was lacking, we received encouragement from the A.O.C.-in-C. of Army Co-operation Command who co-operated with us on an informal basis. There was, for example, an occasion on which he hid a Eureka set in a wood and watched while an aircraft fitted with Rebecca sought and found the hiding place. The lack of early enthusiasm for Eureka and Rebecca serves only to illustrate how disastrous it would have been had this attitude to radar devices been general instead of rare indeed.

As D-Day approached there was no longer any doubt of the attitude of the R.A.F. to Eureka and Rebecca; they needed them and prepared for their use. Moreover, during a visit to Malvern of a number of high-ranking U.S. Army officers, T.R.E. exercised its not always appreciated function of salesmanship; we 'sold' Eureka and Rebecca to the American Army and supplied staff to help the Americans to instal the equipments and to train personnel in their use. When D-Day came, not only British, but American airborne forces were dropped on French soil in weather conditions which would, in many cases, have made visual location impossible.

Miserable weather heralded D-Day but to the radar men it was an opportunity. Because of the distances involved, the familiar artillery barrage put down ahead of advancing troops had to be replaced by a barrage of bombs dropped from the air. But on D-Day, solid cloud stretched across the English Channel and visual bombing would have been impossible. This was a grand opportunity for radar and it did not fail. The barrages were laid accurately by radar control from England and they fell on the defending forces without hurt to the invaders.

When the invasion had been established, there was much work for radar to do; work which continued throughout the march of the armies across France, Belgium and Europe. The tasks of radar were many. Direct support of ground troops, of the kind provided on D-Day, became standard practice. The enemy's air power was rendered negligible with the aid of radar, which provided various forms of ground-controlled interception of hostile fighters and bombers.

Not least of the contributions of radar was the part it played in isolating the battlefield. This is a familiar expression to military men and it means simply the denial to the enemy of the power of reinforcing the area with vehicles and men. The T.R.E. Invasion Panel had not foreseen the radar control of single-seater fighter-bomber aircraft against camouflaged targets in the battle area and most of the credit for this application of radar belongs to the American scientists at T.R.E. The pilot of a single-seater dive-bomber can hardly give much attention to complicated radar equipment and the Americans got over this difficulty by providing radar control from the ground. From a ground-radar station, the position of the dive-bomber could be continuously observed and the pilot of the aircraft was directed by radiotelephony towards a previously located target, often camouflaged tanks or batteries. When he had been directed to a proper position for attack, he was told to dive on to a target which, in all probability, he had not yet seen. The good downward view available in a dive usually enabled the pilot to see the camouflaged target and to attack it. Splendid work of this kind continued throughout the land operations in Europe. I was privileged to hear a talk given by Major-General Quesada to the American scientists at T.R.E., in which he extolled the part that radar had played in the march across Europe. Without radar, he said, the U.S.A. bombing would, because of bad weather, have been largely an 'agricultural blitz'.

This is perhaps the moment to express my admiration of the speed with which the U.S.A. Service personnel and scientists learnt to work together. I have said that one of the factors which led the Americans to set up teams of their scientists at T.R.E. was their recognition that we had evolved an intimate and fruitful association between Service user and laboratory scientist. I think it is true that, in 1943, the Americans had much to learn in this direction, but they learnt with astonishing speed. One incident occurs to my mind. Preparatory to telling me some news of the progress of events in Europe, the leader of one of the two U.S.A. teams of scientists at T.R.E. said to me: 'I was over on the other side yesterday and had lunch with Patton at his Head-quarters.' I remember that, when he left me, my mind wandered back over the long, long road we in England had travelled towards an intimate association between Service personnel and the scientists in their laboratories. I do not think our American colleagues would begrudge me the thought that we had shown them the way.

I shall ever be of the opinion that the greatest contribution made by radar to the success of the invasion of Europe, and indeed to the whole war, was its decisive role in the defeat of the German U-boat fleet. It is surely not arguable that, had not the submarine war been decisively won in 1943, the invasion of Europe could hardly have been successful. It is my personal opinion that it would not even have been attempted. Surely one of the most astonishing facts of the whole war was that, with the Germans in possession of the Bay of Biscay ports, her submarines were unable to take more than a trifling toll of the vast armada which crossed the Atlantic, or of the vaster armada which sailed for Normandy in June 1944.

I have not disguised my opinion that, without radar, the bombing of Germany by our night bombers would have been a costly failure and that, without radar, we should have lost the war at sea. In relation to these great contributions to victory, what part did radar play in the successful invasion of Europe?

We at T.R.E. had made a great deal of fuss about the part we could play when the allied armies landed in Europe. Since 1942 we had been a little disgruntled by apparent lack of interest in the reports prepared by our Invasion Panel. In January 1944, when even the newspapers talked of the coming invasion of northern Europe, no one at T.R.E. had any knowledge of when and where the landings were to be made or of the general plans for the invasion. We had become so accustomed to being taken into the confidence of the R.A.F. Commands on other operations that, rightly or wrongly, we felt that we might have suggestions to make if a few of us could be told of the plans for the coming invasion. Our difficulty was, of course, that the invasion secrets were not the sole property of one Fighting Service, or even of one country. Recognizing this, I arranged a meeting in January 1944 between representatives of all the defence Experimental Establishments working on radar. At this meeting it was agreed that each Establishment, through its Headquarters, should ask that a small number of the staff of each Establishment should be initiated into the plans for D-Day. This method of approach, together with support from Lord

Cherwell, was successful, and in mid-March 1944 three members of T.R.E., together with representatives from other Experimental Establishments, listened to a fascinating talk on the plans for the invasion of northern France. For the purposes of my story, the importance of this event lies not in whether the scientists were able to improve upon the plans that had been made but in acceptance of the fact that scientists at Experimental Establishments were likely to be more fruitful if they were brought into the whole operational story.

There is no simple answer to the question whether our importunity led to important results or indeed to whether radar played a major part in the victory over the German armies in northern Europe. It is certainly true that, after the initiation of the radar scientists into the plans for D-Day, proposals were accepted of a nature which even now cannot be disclosed. In my view, the preparations made for D-Day were on such a gigantic scale that, given average weather conditions, the landings could have been made and bridge-heads established without the use of T.R.E. devices. The weather on 6 June 1944 and on succeeding days could, however, hardly have been more unsuitable; whether Oboe, Gee, Eureka, Rebecca, and other devices made the differ-ence between success and failure is more than anyone can say. I am inclined to think that the landings would in any case have eventually been successful but that radar saved thousands of men's lives. Once the landings had been made and the positions consolidated, it is my view that, although radar greatly reduced our casualties, the defeat of the German armies in their retreat from Normandy to Germany would still have happened had radar not been used.

On the other hand, without radar our invading forces (and those of Russia as well) would have had to face German armies supported by industries which had not been shattered by bombing.

CHAPTER XIX

SOME MEMORIES AND FEATURES
OF T.R.E.

I USED sometimes to say that T.R.E. was an establishment that liked to be visited. Most memorable of all was
the royal visit on 19 July 1944, when we had the honour of
receiving Their Majesties the King and Queen at Malvern
College. After weeks of miserable weather even the sun
shone on that perfect day.

We also had our fair share of visits from distinguished men
and I attached great importance to them. None who were
at T.R.E. will deny that we set ourselves out to give distinguished visitors a field day. Preparations for these visits
meant a lot of extra work when we were already overburdened and the question arises, was the effort worth
while? To answer this question, I will describe what we
tried to give to these visitors and what we hoped to get from
them. As an example, let us consider the first visit to T.R.E.
of a Cabinet minister or of a high-ranking R.A.F. officer and
see first what we tried to give.

The basis of our preparations was a conviction that
scientists at an applied research Establishment ought to be
able to tell a simple story of what they are trying to do and
why they are trying to do it. Any visitor has a right to expect
that this will happen and if, instead, he has to listen to hours
of scientific jargon which he does not understand, he can be
forgiven for not being impressed. It is on this point that
I have a confession to make. Visitors frequently commented
on the clarity of mind and objectivity of those who gave
radar demonstrations to them; the other side of the picture

PLATE VII

THEIR MAJESTIES THE KING AND QUEEN
AT T.R.E., 19 JULY 1944

was that only those who could tell a simple story of their work were chosen for these demonstrations. We sometimes wished we could have a special staff for showing visitors round T.R.E. While discussing this matter one day, I remember Dee saying: 'What we really want, is a verger of a bombed-out cathedral.'

Prior to the visit a programme was arranged, each item being given a certain number of minutes; on special occasions there was a rehearsal on the day preceding the visit. It was a fetish with me that, as far as was humanly possible, no distinguished visitor, other than a scientist, should ever see a poor demonstration. To tell a senior R.A.F. officer that a device was working yesterday, will certainly work tomorrow, but that it is not working to-day, is not the best way to solicit his support. What he remembers of the device is that it did not work. To reduce the risk of failure to an absolute minimum, a member of T.R.E., usually my personal scientific assistant, preceded the main party by a few minutes and therefore became known as John the Baptist. It was his task to verify that the next demonstration was ready and in working order; if it was not, he returned to warn me and the party was steered elsewhere until the trouble was rectified. This was a perfectly legitimate procedure because the visitor was interested in seeing a demonstration of an item of equipment and not in an explanation of how a special valve had blown five minutes ago and of how fast a laboratory assistant was running to get a replacement. With these preliminary explanations, let us see how the visitor spent his day.

First he was taken to my office and shown simple coloured diagrams illustrating the uses of various radar devices. He was also shown charts on which were displayed the operational results obtained with various devices. I first had these drawings made for the visit of a Cabinet minister to Bawdsey before the war and they became known as Politicians' Diagrams. Special drawings prepared for the Royal visit became known as the Royal Diagrams.

Next the visitor was taken to the large assembly hall of the College. This was our Hall of Magic for visitors. In it was kept in readiness for demonstration a sample of almost every radar training device developed at T.R.E. The training devices provided an ideal means of showing the operational uses of our equipment. Without needing the vast equipment and high towers associated with the coastal radar chain, the characteristic echoes of aircraft approaching our coasts were displayed on a cathode-ray tube and visitors were shown the effects of various forms of jamming and of anti-jamming devices. After moving only a few feet, the visitor was shown the first process of night interception. Without the use of aircraft, he was shown the movement of hostile and friendly aircraft across the screen of a Ground Controlled Interception training device and was shown how aircraft tracks could be plotted. The visitor then moved on and was shown various forms of Air Interception training equipment; with these, the visitor had to imagine that he was in a night-fighter aircraft looking at radar indications of an enemy flying ahead. The most realistic, and most complicated, of these devices was largely designed by A. M. Uttley, one of the outstanding men of T.R.E. A darkened room contained a screen illuminated to represent, at will, any condition of night visibility from full moonlight to a dark night with haze. In the centre of the room was the cabin of a night fighter in which the 'crew' sat before radar screens showing indications appropriate to the relative movements of the simulated enemy and fighter aircraft. On to the screen was thrown the silhouette of an enemy bomber, appearing large at close range but disappearing as the range increased. In a demonstration, the visitor at first saw nothing but the movements of the earth's horizon as the fighter crew used their simulated radar indications to overtake the bomber. After a time, the bomber could be seen on the screen and then the fun began. This uncanny trainer could simulate the conditions of an enemy taking violent avoiding action and the efforts of the fighter pilot to get the enemy into his gun-sights could be seen by the onlookers. At last came a simulated rattle of gun-fire from the fighter and the demonstration concluded with the transformation of the bomber into a glowing flame. Needless to say, the bomber was always destroyed in our demonstrations. One more example, that of the H_2S training device, must suffice to show what the visitor saw in our Hall of Magic. On an illuminated glass screen the visitor was shown a map of part of Germany, such as the north-western seaboard. On a cathode-ray screen, a few feet away, he saw the radar indications obtained as a bomber flew over this area; water could be distinguished from land and, by the turn of a knob, towns could be distinguished from countryside. The visitor was usually asked to choose a target for bombing; he would then see the ever-changing radar map on the screen as the bomber approached the target. Finally the release signal was given and the position of the 'bomb' when it reached the ground could be seen on the map of the area. Although we used to say that we could make our fortunes at Blackpool with these devices, they were not toys, nor were they designed for display to visitors. They were a vital factor in the R.A.F.'s training programme and they certainly saved more money, in terms of war effort, than was spent on the whole of T.R.E. throughout the war.

So far, there had been a certain amount of showmanship in the programme. We had tried to show a visitor that the experiments he was yet to see were not a game for the amusement of scientists but a vital part of the whole war effort. Now the character of the programme changed and the visitor was shown samples of the whole work of T.R.E. He was given demonstrations of new devices in various stages of development and was shown through laboratories, workshops and drawing offices. The aim of this part of the programme was to show T.R.E. as it really was; its people, its size and its facilities. Of course the whole of T.R.E. could not be shown; this would have involved a visit of three days. If the visitor showed particular interest in knowing how radar devices worked, he was taken to our film unit and shown speech films made for training purposes. Sometimes a visit to T.R.E. was combined with a visit to T.F.U. at Defford, where radar devices installed in aircraft could be seen, but T.F.U. was worthy of a separate visit.

At the end of the day the visitor and senior members of T.R.E. gathered together in my office and, over a much-needed mug of tea, there was generally a free and often stimulating discussion on T.R.E. in particular and on the war in general.

I have tried to show what we had to give a visitor and it remains to tell why we gave gladly. First, I believed that distinguished visitors should be seen by as many T.R.E. people as possible; they could give by their very presence. The senior scientific men were, of course, not in need of stimulants of this kind; they would have been dull indeed had they not known of the importance of our tasks. But the majority of the T.R.E. personnel were not scientists or technicians and it was harder for them to believe that we had a special mission in the war. If, however, a Cabinet minister, or an R.A.F. Commander-in-Chief in the middle of a battle, could be seen walking through key departments such as the workshops, an outward and visible sign of the importance of our tasks was demonstrated to all. The second reason why we welcomed distinguished visitors was that we usually wanted something. We might need more staff or more buildings, or we might want to tell a high-ranking R.A.F. officer our views on the need for some new radar device or on how an existing device could be more profitably used. It was said once in London that 'If you let an Air Marshal get near T.R.E. they will sell him anything.' All I need say is that it was our job to sell.

All these carefully planned arrangements did not, of course, apply to visiting scientists such as Tizard and Lord Cherwell, who gladly took pot-luck on the availability of equipment for demonstrations. It must be admitted, too, that there was at least one exception to the ease with which a carefully planned programme was carried through. Most of our visitors kept, with some prompting, to a timed schedule they carried with them, but Sir Archibald Sinclair defeated us. His interest in the detail of demonstrations, and in those giving them, was so great that irretrievable arrears of time soon accumulated and the end of the programme inevitably suffered. It was not until the last visit of this friend and great supporter of ours that we evolved a method of dealing with the situation. We simply did not give Sir Archibald a copy of the programme and so were free to arrange that, by omitting some items, the most important were not missed.

I have given special attention to the carefully planned visits of distinguished men partly because they were not always understood and partly because it is perhaps not obvious that an applied research Establishment gains from them what it is prepared to put into them. These special visitors were, of course, a minority. The normal work of the Establishment profited greatly from visits, numbering thousands per year, from representatives from Head-quarters, Industry, Service Commands and Units, other Experimental Establishments and from Universities.

It is my belief that only one important visit, that of press representatives at the end of the German war, was a dismal failure. We made special preparations for it, believing that the taxpayer who provided the money for our work should know what T.R.E. had done and should know something of the personnel and facilities needed to achieve results in applied research. We showed them all that Cabinet ministers and other distinguished visitors had seen, including the Hall of Magic, but we failed to impress more than a few of them. While demonstrations were being given, some stayed in the background exchanging stories which were apparently funny. Others were interested in what radar might do in the future but not at all in what had been done in the past. Happily, some of the press representatives clearly wanted to learn all they could, but, on this visit, I was left with a sense of failure without understanding its cause.

If this were a history of radar instead of one story of one radar experimental Establishment, a volume would be needed to describe the contributions made to radar by the Headquarters staffs of the M.A.P. and of the Air Ministry. The Headquarters organization responsible for the work of T.R.E. changed its character a number of times during the war but it will suffice here to give a picture of T.R.E. as responsible to a Director of Communications Development in M.A.P., who was responsible to a Controller of Communications Equipment. The Air Ministry was not, in theory, responsible for the work of T.R.E. but, in practice, the Director-General of Signals had a great influence on our affairs. Moreover, on communications equipment, the M.A.P. and the Air Ministry were linked, in the later stages of the war, by the duality of the office of Controller of Communications Equipment (M.A.P.) and the Controller of Communications (Air Ministry). In addition, Sir Robert Watson-Watt held an Advisory post with the Air Ministry.

There are curiously conflicting views on the subject of the relationship between a London Headquarters and an applied research Establishment. Some University scientists, with little experience of Government research, seem to believe that Experimental Establishments have simply to do what Headquarters tells them to do and, since control of University research from an office in London would rightly be anathema to them, they imagine that scientists at a Government research Establishment are mere slaves. At T.R.E. this viewpoint would have been ridiculed but the danger exists that young University graduates may believe it to be true.

On the other hand, there are those at Experimental Establishments who believe that a Headquarters Organization, if needed at all, should be subservient to Experimental Establishments. In one sense this latter viewpoint is a legitimate one. For breaking new ground, even in applied science, what is most needed is knowledge and I am in no doubt that the most knowledgeable scientists are, or should be, in or alongside the laboratories. It follows that all who do administrative work, whether at Headquarters or as Heads of Experimental Establishments, should feel themselves to be in large measure the servants of the working scientists.

We at T.R.E. regarded Headquarters and our Establishment as complementary, each taking a dominant role in different fields of effort. Our broad understanding of the needs of the air-war was derived from our contacts with the Director-General of Signals and from our more informal contacts with the R.A.F. Commands, while a more detailed and intimate picture was obtained from contacts with operational Squadrons and in this our Post-Design Services helped greatly. Proposals for radar solutions of war problems usually came from the working scientists in the laboratories, which is what one would expect. Work on a new radar device could be initiated at T.R.E. without reference to Headquarters, it being left to us to use a sense of proportion in this matter. Decisions on whether a promising device should be developed and produced by Industry were made at meetings at which M.A.P. Headquarters, the R.A.F. user and T.R.E. were represented. Sometimes these meetings were in London and sometimes decisions of this kind were, in effect, taken at our Sunday Soviets. There was often plenty of noise at these meetings but they almost always ended in substantial unanimity on what should be done; moreover they served to kill unfruitful ideas in their infancy.

Up to this stage in the evolution of a new radar device, it is probably true to say that T.R.E. had been the leading partner in the Headquarters-T.R.E. combination, but now M.A.P. Headquarters assumed the dominant role. Decisions had to be made on what firm or firms should make the main equipment and its associated test-gear and on what quantities would be needed by specified dates. These decisions having been made, Headquarters was faced with a great deal of exacting work in arranging contracts and in watching the progress of a production programme which was often rendered complicated by successive modifications. A decision to fit a new radar device into specified types of aircraft also called for important and difficult discussions between Headquarters and the aircraft Industry. Air Ministry Headquarters was also faced with new tasks. Additional man-power might have to be found and trained to operate the device or, for radar in aircraft, the already overburdened crews had to be trained in new methods. Viewing the position as a whole, we can be thankful that, early in the war, M.A.P. Headquarters, Air Ministry and T.R.E. settled down into a state of acknowledgement of the roles of all concerned.

The choice of the men who occupied the most important Headquarters positions during the most critical years of the war was particularly fortunate for T.R.E. The first Controller was Sir Frank Smith, who occupied the post during the grand Swanage era, when fantastic conceptions turned rapidly into practicable schemes. His understanding of the ways of scientists was of inestimable value to our work. During the later stages of the war, when new ideas mattered less than a ruthless exploitation of existing ones, the Controller was Sir Robert Renwick, who brought his business experience and his energy to bear on the massive problem of ensuring that our devices became available in quantity to the R.A.F. During this period the Director of Communications Development was Air Commodore Leedham whose organizing ability and detailed knowledge of the radio Industry was indispensable. Lastly, but far from least, Watson-Watt in his advisory capacity on communications was a constant source of strength to us. He was, I suppose, our most frequent visitor and became as much one of us as his Headquarters post allowed him to be.

I have described the relations between Headquarters and T.R.E. because of the harmful theory, prevalent in some quarters, that first-class scientists in an Establishment working on defence problems will be crushed by dictatorial orders from London. I feel it important to stress that nothing of the kind happened at T.R.E. Of course, if an Experimental Establishment is not sufficiently productive of new ideas to make its own programme, it must expect others to tell it exactly what to do.

Viewing the position as a whole, after experience at both junior and senior levels at Headquarters and in Experimental Establishments, my personal view is that, for good or ill, Experimental Establishments have a greater opportunity for influencing events than Headquarters. For this reason nearly all of the best scientific men should be in the field and not in London.

At the end of the German war there were between two and three hundred American scientists, technicians and administrative staff within the barbed-wire confines of T.R.E. It is not my business to describe the work of the two American teams which shared Malvern College with us. Their work was controlled by their parent Establishments in the U.S.A. and by the American authorities in the European theatre of operations. These two teams served the American Armed Forces in Europe as we served the R.A.F. Neither is it my business to describe the close co-operation between the British and the Americans on all radar problems. Suffice it here to say that the need for this co-operation was obvious: both countries had to face the threat of the U-boats, both were concerned with the bombing of Germany and the armies of the two countries were to march side by side across western Europe. Co-operation on radar had begun as early as August 1940 when, at the Prime Minister's invitation, Tizard took a mission to the United States. This mission told the American authorities of our progress in radar and they gave the U.S.A. the priceless gift of a magnetron.

In the summer of 1943 T.R.E. was visited by an important American mission consisting of senior officers of the Navy and Army and of distinguished scientists. This mission was impressed with the facilities at Malvern College, with the vast flying facilities available to us at T.F.U. at Defford which exceeded anything then contemplated for scientists in their own country, and they were impressed with the intimate and informal co-operation between Service user and civilian scientists which had been built up at T.R.E. The mission freely admitted that the degree of co-operation achieved exceeded anything they had thought possible. I do not know whether the mission then had in mind putting American scientists at Malvern College; I certainly suggested it to them and I expect many others made the same proposal. At any rate, late in the summer of 1943, the American teams began to arrive and T.R.E. never again looked quite the same place.

The American scientists brought a freshness and gaiety to their tasks which we were beginning to lack, perhaps because they had not passed through a grim period of probable defeat. They worked as hard as any but managed at the same time to seem like schoolboys having an unexpected holiday. The establishment of the American scientists at T.R.E. worked perfectly. We shared each other's secrets and discussed each other's problems. We tried to provide them with any facilities for their work which they did not possess and I have no knowledge that we failed. I still marvel that men of different nationalities got on so well. During the two years they were with us, not a single case of friction between British and American personnel came to my notice. At first we were a little cautious in our approaches to one another. Long afterwards, I learnt that we had each been given the same advice about the other. Both had been said to be lacking in a sense of humour, to be a little sensitive and to need tactful handling. I can only speak from my experience at T.R.E., but I found this advice to be nonsense. Soon the peculiarities of each of our countries were the source of jests which did much to cement friendship. My chief regret was that the intensity of our lives prohibited much social contact, but we had our moments. There was, for example, an occasion on which I challenged the Americans to play a cricket match against a T.R.E. team of men over forty, the result to decide whether the U.S.A. joined the British Commonwealth of Nations or whether the United Kingdom became the Forty-Ninth State. The British team won but the Americans, wanting to regain their nationality, challenged us to a game of baseball in which the challengers were to play left-handed. It is sad to relate that, by keeping us in ignorance of the rules of the game, the Americans regained their nationality.

When the German war ended, the lively farewell parties which each gave the other were, for me, tinged with sadness. I was glad when the Americans came and sorry when they left. They gave much to us and I think we gave something to them.

I do not propose to describe in detail the organization of T.R.E., which frequently changed with changing needs, but it may be useful to record some of the more permanent features of the Establishment and to consider whether a research Establishment needs an organization in the generally accepted sense. There are those who seem to deprecate any sign of tidiness in the conduct of research matters. On the other hand there are those who seek to find at a research Establishment a rigid organization of the vertical pattern, in which every scientist is paid in accordance with the number of staff immediately responsible to him. I can only give my own views in this matter, for what they are worth. When a research Establishment has a total strength of about 100 people there is little need to rely on written rules of conduct governing the work of the scientists and the acquisition of facilities for them. Everybody knows everybody else and any Head of the Establishment who is worthy of the title will run his staff through the medium of frequent personal contacts. When however an Establishment attains a strength of thousands, and particularly when its work becomes increasingly of an applied character, there must either be some measure of tidiness and adherence to circulated

186

instructions, or chaos. Personal contacts between the Head of an Establishment and its personnel are still vital but a simple example will suffice to show their practical limitations. At T.R.E. I made it known that any member of the Establishment could see me by appointment if he had a grievance or personal worry which his immediate superiors had failed to dispel. In particular, I made it known that any man or woman who felt that he was not given opportunity to work at his maximum capacity or who was working without being told why his work was needed, could come direct to me. If, in an Establishment of 3,000 people, every man and woman had sought my personal intervention once each year, I should have had an average of ten such cases every working day. Clearly this would have been an impossible situation. Thus, in a large Establishment, there must be a mechanism which, for want of a more palatable word, we call organization; a mechanism which provides for devolved and redevolved responsibilities and for a more or less uniform standard of conduct and procedure regarding security, acquisition of stores, demands upon drawing offices and workshops and a hundred other matters which form the daily life of a large applied research Establishment. The first step in providing an organization or mechanism for the conduct of T.R.E. was for its senior members to agree on a definition of the policy of the Establishment. No one at T.R.E. attempted to write such a definition but it would have been a simple matter to do so. The policy was to concentrate upon the needs of the war without consideration of the future of the Establishment or of its personnel after the war. (As one member of T.R.E. once put it, we should aim to drop dead to a man on the day of victory.) Within this broad policy, we aimed to keep the secrets of our devices from the enemy and to conform to the principle that the Establishment was ultimately responsible to Parliament, through

Headquarters, for the expenditure of the considerable funds provided for its work. It is to be feared that we regarded this latter duty as a rightful rendering unto Caesar of the things that were Caesar's.

It remains to tell how the policy was disseminated throughout the Establishment. If it is true, as I believe it is, that any research Establishment can be killed by the adoption of a dictatorial attitude from Headquarters, it is equally true that a dictatorial Head of an Establishment will achieve the same result. The first step in the organization of a large Establishment is, therefore, to set up an internal governing body. At T.R.E. this need was met by the somewhat erroneously named Divisional Leaders Meetings which were attended by the Superintendents and Divisional Leaders who were responsible for the work of large scientific staffs, by Jones, who was responsible for finance, stores and a host of other administrative matters, by Gregory, who controlled the Drawing Offices and Workshops, and by V. F. Knight, who was responsible for security, welfare, accommodation and general amenities. At these meetings we discussed everything that was our business and much that was not. Subjects of discussion ranged from the conduct of the war to the food in the canteen. Every member of T.R.E. knew that he could raise a matter for his Divisional Leader to discuss at these meetings, which were of a most intimate and informal character. It was a golden rule that nothing said at these meetings should be quoted elsewhere. I fear I have not the skill to provide a word picture of the Divisional Leaders meetings though they remain a vivid memory. I have never listened to a higher standard of objective discussion or of humour than it was my privilege to hear on these occasions. These meetings provided the first step in the process of devolution, in that a dozen or more men shared complete knowledge of our common hopes and fears, of our enemies and our friends and of our successes and our failures. The next step was for each Divisional Leader to hold meetings of his few Group Leaders, men who were responsible for from ten to thirty scientific staff. These meetings dealt with the work of the Divisions and were followed by discussions. The process of dissemination among the scientific staff was completed by Group Leaders holding regular meetings of a similar character. These meetings at various levels provided a channel whereby the internal policy regarding the conduct of our affairs percolated throughout the scientific staff.

Most of the T.R.E. personnel were not, however, scientists and it was vital that those who served the scientists should share the sources of inspiration open to the laboratory workers and, within the limits imposed by security, should understand how their work fitted into the needs of the war. The handling of these matters for the several hundreds of industrial personnel employed in our workshops will serve as an example. In addition to representation by Gregory at the informal Divisional Leaders meetings, regular use was made of the Whitley Council industrial machinery. Meetings of a more informal character were sometimes held to discuss our domestic workshop problems and a Production Committee met at regular intervals. I have little to say on this subject except that no body of men and women of equal size caused me less trouble. During the Establishment's history the workshops were fortunate in being controlled by men like J. E. Airey, J. Sieger and J. Morley who succeeded in forming a happy team with the men and women in the shops. For those knowledgeable on industrial matters it will suffice to say that our absentee rate, for men, other than through sickness, did not rise above 1 per cent for long periods. With sickness it averaged about 3 per cent. I am sure that an important factor in maintaining a good spirit in the shops was the fullest possible disclosure of the purpose of the jobs being worked upon and subsequently of the successes obtained with particular devices. Unreasonable secrecy is as big a cause of inefficiency in workshops as it is in the laboratories.

I am conscious that my story of the organization of T.R.E. appears to err on the side of tidiness. In particular I am anxious to avoid any suggestion that the Head of the Establishment imposed his will upon Divisional Leaders, who, in successive stages, saw that the whole Establishment conformed thereto. It was not like that at all. I am convinced that no research Establishment can be alive without a sprinkling of men having outstanding qualities amounting sometimes to genius. At T.R.E. there were eventually about a dozen such and unless the bulk of these men agreed on some measure of organization, it was useless to put it into effect over a long period. Of course there were occasions when an unpopular procedure later became popular. One such was the scheme of summarizing correspondence which became an important feature of T.R.E. Almost every letter on a technical subject was summarized and a document containing the summaries was circulated to every Group Leader; the document showed clearly who had to take action. Non-technical personnel, preferably possessing more than average feminine charm, were then used to 'chase' the scientists until the letters were answered. At first few liked being chased, but the scheme was later found to relieve the scientists of routine paper work and to allow for lapses of memory. Moreover, at little cost, the Establishment gained a reputation for answering letters.

The essence of the matter is this. A large research Establishment, if it is to be alive and productive, must be organized round the personalities and attributes of the outstanding men it succeeds in recruiting. If the result looks tidy so much the better, but if it looks untidy it cannot be helped. These key men must work together on a basis of mutual respect which the Head of the Establishment should seek unceasingly to foster. One other word regarding the Head of the Establishment. If he is a genius himself, it is most unlikely that he will give adequate attention to the running of a large applied research Establishment, for this is a whole-time task. If he is not a genius, he must recognize that, in spite of the dictatorial noises he may occasionally make, his first duty is to be a servant of his staff and particularly of its outstanding members.

The population of T.R.E. was multiplied twenty times during seven years and it is proper to consider some of the problems that arose in its recruitment. To preserve a balanced Establishment, a growing T.R.E. had to recruit first-class experienced scientists, young and inexperienced University graduates, technical assistants both experienced and inexperienced, clerical staff, designers and draughtsmen, skilled and semi-skilled workshop personnel and unskilled labour.

During the early stages of the war, most of the experienced scientists at the Universities and elsewhere were distributed in accordance with the prevailing needs of the war. We at T.R.E. grumbled about the proportion of first-class men allotted to us but, looking back on it all, we had our fair share. As however the years went on and the vital role of T.R.E. in the war became more apparent, it was clear that we were rapidly accumulating too many inexperienced men in proportion to the almost negligible recruitment of experienced scientists. Of course the younger men originally with us had a golden opportunity but there was a natural limit to the growth of their capacity for leadership. Thus, as early as 1942, the strain on the few first-class scientists was becoming apparent. It was at this time that a member of

M.A.P. Headquarters, after visiting T.R.E., wrote me a letter asking whether I would welcome an examination of the senior T.R.E. scientists by a psychiatrist in disguise! In normal times I should have regarded this proposal as a grand jest to be shared by all, and it is now difficult for me to believe that I was so anxious myself about the strain which the senior scientists were undergoing that I said nothing to them about the letter until long afterwards. My reply was that we needed help from experienced scientists and not a psychiatrist. As a result of pressure from T.R.E., and with the help of Lord Cherwell, an investigation of our needs was made by Lord Hankey and Dr C. P. Snow. It was obvious that, if T.R.E. was to be given more experienced scientists, other Establishments would have to give them up, and the investigators had therefore a difficult task before them. I recall one amusing incident during Lord Hankey's visit. Lord Hankey, Snow and several of the senior T.R.E. men were sitting in my office after dinner when hasty footsteps were heard on the spiral staircase leading to my room. There entered the bearer of a message telling us that the long-feared listening of the enemy to our $1\frac{1}{2}$ m. A.S.V. had begun. We all knew that this meant a more intensive effort on centimetre A.S.V. and the need for still more staff. Long afterwards Snow told me that Lord Hankey would have given much to know on that evening whether the incident had been arranged for his benefit. I am happy to assure him that it was not pre-arranged. Lord Hankey, than whom there is no greater friend of scientists at high level, recommended that about twenty senior experienced scientists should be directed to T.R.E. They came, and several stayed to fill important posts in the Establishment; in particular, tribute should be paid to the B.B.C. for their generous attitude to us. Some of the directed scientists had, however, been used to a more rigid organization than we encouraged at T.R.E. and it was clear that only a return to their accustomed surroundings would put them out of the misery which was their unhappy lot at T.R.E.

It is not to be supposed that all of the senior scientists at T.R.E. were satisfied with the number of newly recruited experienced scientists allotted to them and I remember one amusing protest. Cockburn, whose eloquence was apt to bring a tear to the eye, had been in the forefront during the investigations into our staff needs; when however the new staff arrived, their distribution was based on the needs of the war and not on the degree of eloquence displayed before the investigators. It was with some justification that Cockburn said: 'I am the ferret put down the hole to get the rabbits out and when they come out I am put back in the bag.'

Recruitment of young inexperienced men from the Universities was a more simple matter. The allocation of these young men to the different Ministries was largely in the hands of F. Brundrett at the Admiralty. This was a completely illogical arrangement but, because of Brundrett's scrupulous fairness, it worked well. The problem was not so much to find the young scientific recruits as to turn them into useful members of T.R.E. at the earliest possible moment. It is in general true that a charwoman is more immediately useful to a research Establishment than a young recruit fresh from a University. We largely solved the problem by sending them to the T.R.E. school for several weeks. There they were taught the principles of radar, told the history and purpose of the Establishment and generally brought into the T.R.E. family before being sent to the laboratories. Moreover, an examination was held at the end of the course and those who were found unsuitable were not employed at T.R.E. I attach great importance to the training of recruits before they are let loose in the laboratories where busy men are liable to ignore them if they are not immediately useful.

It may be wondered how, in the fourth year of a war, we were able to recruit hundreds of skilled industrials for our Engineering Unit. We were certainly given the essential high priority for our work but this alone would not have sufficed. We had splendid help from the President of the Worcestershire Man-Power Board but this sufficed only to obtain the men and not to keep them. I like to think that a powerful factor in building up our large Engineering Unit was that Gregory and his staff did everything possible to make the men and women employed in the workshops happy in their work and in their surroundings.

For the rest, we relied largely on local recruitment. Both at Swanage and at Malvern we were the largest employer of labour in the district. There was work for men past their prime, work for cooks and kitchen staff and work for small girls who carried our precious secret papers from House to House in Malvern College. I was often worried about the security of our secrets but one incident made me feel that perhaps my worries were needless. After the cleaner who tidied my office had been with us for three years he came to me one day at Malvern and described a great discovery he had made during a holiday in Swanage. 'Do you know', he said, 'that they have a gadget at Swanage which tells them when enemy aircraft are coming to attack us?'

It is my belief that there are two dangers to the scientific health of an applied research Establishment. One is that it will produce nothing new and will sink to the level of performing moderately useful but mediocre tasks. The other is that it will be supremely successful in initiating new equipments and will die from the resulting burden imposed upon the Establishment. None can deny that we at T.R.E. evolved new devices which had a decisive effect upon the outcome of the war but perhaps few realize that, as a research

Establishment, we were almost bankrupt at the end of the war.

Whether from conceit or from other human frailties is beyond analysis but we at T.R.E. certainly believed that we had a special mission to perform, and that victory depended in no mean degree upon our efforts. Whatever our failings, which were many, the senior men at T.R.E. concentrated upon the needs of the war without thought of the future of the Establishment or of its personnel. Lest it be thought that we possessed some special brand of altruism, let us remember that most of the senior T.R.E. scientists had no interest in what happened to T.R.E. after the war; their concern was to help to finish the war as soon as possible and to return to fundamental research at the Universities.

I am in no doubt that the gradual process of decay of T.R.E. as a research Establishment was in the best interests of the war. Viewing the history of the Establishment from 1935, it is more nearly true to say that there had been two periods of decay, one of which has already been described. Some splendid applied research had been done at Orfordness and at Bawdsey but gradually the bulk of the small staff became immersed, at the sacrifice of research, in the physical task of erecting the coastal chain for the coming Battle of Britain. The dispersal of the staff at the outbreak of war and the lack of facilities for research at Dundee brought about the temporary bankruptcy already described.

The second period of decay was more obvious to us at T.R.E. and perhaps less apparent to others. I am in no doubt that, considering T.R.E. as an applied research Establishment, our greatest days were at Swanage. When the newly recruited eminent scientists had combined with the pre-war staff still with us to form something like a team, we lived through an era of radar miracles. Wherever one looked, something new was being evolved. In particular, the early work on centimetre radar coloured a period of applied research through which it was a privilege to live. Unfortunately for applied research, and fortunately for the progress of the war, the Swanage era also saw the sowing of the seeds of our decay as a research Establishment. We came in this era to know that science and the mere demonstration of new devices were not enough and, as has been described in Chapter x, we initiated methods of reducing the time interval between a scientific demonstration of a device and its full availability to the R.A.F. and methods for aiding the R.A.F. to use and to maintain the new equipment. Almost imperceptibly at first, the character of the Establishment changed until, at the end of the war, only a minority of the scientific staff was engaged on work which could be called research.

For two reasons some research, which we called basic work, was conducted towards future types of radar and associated equipment. Before D-Day, and until it was certain that the end in Europe was only a matter of time, we at T.R.E. sometimes discussed, in our informal way, what ought to be done if the invasion failed. Certain ideas were forthcoming, which we called plan B; ideas which depended upon the success of basic research work. I must emphasize that I have no knowledge of the plans which would have been put into operation had the invasion of northern France been a failure. Plan B had no existence outside Malvern but it at least provided us with a reason for letting some basic research be done. The other reason for permitting some research work to go on was the excellent one that it was good for what remained of our souls.

In proportion to the great scientific strength of T.R.E., however, the amount of basic work was pathetically small and, in the interests of the war, T.R.E. suffered a decay as a research Establishment which was obvious to us all. I am convinced that, in time of peace, research workers who evolve radar and other equipment should not be burdened for years with the subsequent history of their devices. It is preferable that some of the best research workers should not even be responsible for the first design of their devices in practical form. Others, and perhaps the majority of research workers, should see their projects through only to the stage of approval of a manufacturer's prototype. No first-rate scientist with ideas should be concerned in time of peace with manuals and schedules and with minor modifications to the children of his brain. These men should be encouraged, whether they like it or not, to leave this work to engineers who will do it better, thus allowing the scientists freedom to explore fresh fields. Our inability in war to put these principles into practice constituted the first of three reasons for our decay as a research Establishment.

The second reason for the decay of T.R.E. as a research Establishment was its ever-growing size. It is not an accident that the majority of fundamental advances in science have been made by small teams in Universities and elsewhere. It is idle to suppose that there is any comparison between the organization of a University research team and that of an Establishment of 3,000 people in which technical men, down to the lowest grade, form the minority and in which not more than one in a hundred of the personnel is a first-class scientist. A small team of scientists can be run on a basis of personal knowledge of each other and with a minimum of paper work. A body of 3,000 people, whether it be an army unit or a research Establishment, must inevitably be governed by rules and regulations which, although necessary to prevent chaos, will rob first-rate scientists of some of the freedom essential to their work. It will sometimes happen that a research Establishment of thousands of people is inevitable. For example, modern aerodynamical research involves wind-tunnel equipment of such prodigious cost that it cannot be made available to every small team that may need it. Thus a large scientific staff will tend to grow around the costly equipment. Moreover, research on aero-dynamics and on propulsion units for aircraft is rapidly merging into one study, with the result that the number of scientific workers at one Establishment tends still further to be large. My only plea is that, wherever possible, a research Establishment should be small enough to constitute a family which conducts its affairs on a basis of accepted customs and not on written rules and regulations. In my view only exceptional circumstances justify an Establishment being larger than 500, including the cleaners.

The third reason for the decay of T.R.E. as a research Establishment was that many, including most of the key men, gradually lost their freshness and, at the end of the war, were dead tired. Even in the Swanage era I was approached by local medical men who considered that many of the staff were in danger of nervous breakdowns. By the end of the war, the result of years of strain was all too apparent. I do not believe that the strain on the leading scientific men was primarily associated with long hours of work since I have little doubt that many of them had worked equally long hours in their pre-war University lives. I believe that the strain was partly due to a knowledge of the awful price to be paid for failure to achieve radar solutions of some of the major war problems and partly to their unavoidably uncongenial tasks. By the end of the war they were indeed far from doing work of the kind they believed they had been born to do. Two examples of the atmosphere of T.R.E. in the latter days of the war must suffice. I have a mental picture of Dee in 1940, surrounded by equipment which seemed to bear little relation to the needs of the current war; he, with Skinner and others, was breaking new ground and was delighted to receive an echo with centimetre equipment from a man on a bicycle. I have also a mental picture of Dee in 1945. He had descended, when not attending meetings in London, to sitting in an office with two telephones, often ringing at once. Files dealing with dates for meeting our commitments, with modifications and other unscientific matters, littered his desk, and there was always his Secretary to give him more paper if he should be seen for a moment to revert to the luxury of thinking. I have used Dee as an example, but most of the senior scientists suffered in the same way. The great contribution these men made to the war effort is not to be reckoned only by the devices they evolved but by their willingness to forsake their professions when the needs of the war called for consolidation rather than for new ideas.

A second example of the changed atmosphere at T.R.E. is provided by the nature of the almost daily telephone calls between the Controller of Communications Equipment, Sir Robert Renwick, and myself. 'Have you', Renwick used to say, 'any news?' This question was a constant reminder to me of how far T.R.E. had travelled since it was a research Establishment. I used sometimes to wonder what a University research leader would say if he were telephoned from London almost every day and asked for news of the progress he had made. Renwick, of course, was right, and we were right to put research in the background when what mattered most was to deliver to the R.A.F. the results of earlier research in usable form. On the whole none can say that the timing of the change of T.R.E. from a research Establishment to a purveyor of devices for use in the war was much in error.

I have been concerned to describe the decay of T.R.E. as a research Establishment because as long as the reasons for decay are understood, resuscitation is always possible, and indeed not difficult, once the causes are removed. For the reasons I have given, hardly a new idea was evolved at T.R.E. during the last year of the war. This was unimportant. What is important is that no research Establishment should continue to work almost exclusively on bread-and-butter matters when the reason for doing so, such as war, has been removed. It is good to know that all concerned with the post-war fate of T.R.E. understood these matters and that T.R.E. has been saved from a fate which its successes might have brought upon it.

CHAPTER XX

CONCLUSION

I HAVE tried to tell a simple story of T.R.E. from when it was a handful of men working at Orfordness until its 3,000 men and women, Service and civilian, swarmed in and around Malvern College and Defford aerodrome. It is far from being a complete story and I doubt whether it is even a balanced story such as might be produced from an exhaustive examination of the Establishment's records. I have tried, however, to show something of T.R.E. as it really was from 1935 to the end of the war. Were I writing fiction, an elementary sense of drama would lead me to describe T.R.E. as ending its wartime history in a blaze of glory and endeavour such as soldiers may experience on the day of victory; but for T.R.E. there was no such end of the war. At the end of Chapter XIX I have described some of the reasons which led to the gradual decay of T.R.E. as a research Establishment, but for the last few months of the war there was another reason for a changing atmosphere. It was that we were no longer very important to the outcome of either the German or the Japanese wars. With the allied armies sweeping into Germany, the end of the German war was in sight and if T.R.E. had been swallowed in a night it would hardly have delayed victory by an hour. The position was not much different for the Japanese war. Only one or two of the senior T.R.E. men believed in a long war against Japan. We were certainly busy enough in modifying our equipments to render them serviceable under tropical conditions and in designing special radar equipments to meet the operational conditions of the Far East. In May 1945 we sent to India a party of scientists under Taylor to assist the local R.A.F. authorities with their radar problems. But it was clear to most of us that the Japanese war presented no new radar tasks of the magnitude which had faced us in the past. There was no mystery about our declining importance. There is a phase difference between research and its application to war. We had been effectively at war since 1935 and it was natural that we should have little influence on events during the closing stages.

Signs of our decreasing importance were not lacking. Many of the leaders of T.R.E. who had given it its special character were rightly taken from us for more important work or returned to their sadly neglected Universities. Visitors became fewer and even the Sunday Soviets lost their purpose.

There were a few who rebelled against the scattering of the men who controlled the destinies of T.R.E. I remember, in particular, one superintendent at the Establishment who, as was his way, paced up and down my office pleading that it was easier to destroy the team that had been built up than to create another and that we ought to offer ourselves, as a team, for some major post-war task. I could not share his view. Our special task was over and it was right that many of the senior men should return to the Universities and to Industry to prepare for the needs of peace. Moreover, we had lived for too long on our emotions. T.R.E. could live and it could be a better Establishment than it had ever been, but I was convinced that it had to be different, with new leaders and new purposes.

I have tried to show something of the lives we lived ànd something of the magnitude of our belief that we held the key to victory. We believed that without radar Fighter Command and the 'famous few' would have lost the Battle of Britain. We believed that without radar the night attacks by enemy bombers would have devastated our industries. We believed that without radar the work and gallantry of Bomber Command would have been largely wasted; and we believed that without radar the sea-war would have been lost and that there would have been no invasion of Europe. Writing this concluding chapter early in 1947, it already seems impossible that we had such an overwhelming belief in the magnitude of our influence on the outcome of the war. Already our talk of victory being won on the playing fields of Malvern savours of a thin jest; yet it is less than two years since we believed it to be true. Was it true? None can say with certainty, though there were distinguished men outside T.R.E. who thought so. I cannot bring myself to quote more than one opinion on the contribution to victory made by T.R.E. In a letter to me after the German war had ended, Sir Stafford Cripps wrote: 'I do not hesitate to say that without your team we should certainly not be celebrating the victory in Europe—yet—and probably never.'

But if it be true that the T.R.E. scientists played a great part in the successes of the Royal Air Force, it is equally true that, because of its treatment of scientists, the Royal Air Force deserved the aid which science provided. Senior R.A.F. officers, with very few exceptions, brought us fully into their problems and we were never denied a hearing. I remember an occasion when T.R.E. strongly disapproved of the methods of use of one of its devices by Bomber Command. Service matters were involved and we might have been told to mind our business. It was a simple matter, however, to arrange for a meeting, under the Chairmanship of the Deputy Chief of the Air Staff, at which Bomber Command and T.R.E. were given equal opportunity to put their views. Who was in the right is now of no importance; what is important is that scientists at an Experimental Establishment were given a hearing at high level on a matter which involved criticism of the use by the R.A.F. of their equipment.

There are young scientists who fear that to do research work for one of the Fighting Services involves the probability that they, who are civilians by choice and nature, will be browbeaten by men in uniform. I can only say that this has not been my experience. The days are long since gone when a scientist waited outside the door until he was allowed the privilege of making his contribution at a policy meeting, after which he was speedily ushered out. They will only return if an inadequate number of good scientists fails to choose defence research as a career.

One other factor may contribute to the reluctance of scientists to work on defence problems. There has arisen a popular conception that modern science has added to the bloodiness of war. This is surely a superficial view. In 1914 and again in 1939 we were forced to fight a major war. In the first war the British Empire lost a million of its finest men; some of those killed in the trenches were scientists who might have reduced this holocaust. In the Battle of the Somme the British casualties were nearly half a million. The British losses during the first four years of the second war were less than those caused by road accidents in the United Kingdom during the same period.

None can doubt that the vast difference in the casualties of the two wars was due largely to the different attitudes adopted to science and to scientists. For example, before the allied armies fought their way into Germany, German industries and the German power and will to fight had largely been destroyed by a relatively small number of gallant British and American airmen aided by radar.

With our depleted man-power, we are conscious enough of the difficulties of maintaining our place among the great nations. Without the full use of science in the war, the depletion of our man-power would have presented problems beyond hope of solution.

Had there been a scientist in the Victory Parade, he might well have carried on his banner the inscription: 'My profession saved a million lives.'

EPILOGUE

At the end of the war I left T.R.E. and a year after, on the eve of sailing for Australia, I was again in Malvern. It was evening when I walked through the now unguarded gates of Malvern College, into the now empty Main Building, up the spiral staircase to what was once my office and across to the east window. It all looked the same, except that no one was to be seen.

Foolishly, perhaps, I tried to recapture some of the moments I had known at T.R.E.; moments when I had heard of new devices and methods for use against our enemies; moments when I had heard of first operational successes with radar devices, making victory over the submarine and the devastation of Germany as certain as anything can be in war; moments when I knew that I was but one of a hundred men ashamed to admit utter weariness; preparations for D-Day and the misery of hearing the north wind whistling its way towards the Normandy beaches; and then the Victory Service in the Chapel.

I tried hard to think of these things but my mind rejected them. This office had known the contest of wills and the fun of Divisional Leaders' meetings and had known the clamour of Sunday Soviets, but little of these things would come clearly to my mind. Then I understood. It was to this east window that I had gone when, one after the other, many of the key men, British and American, had said good-bye to me when their tasks were done. I recalled that, standing there, I had gone over in my mind what each had given to T.R.E. and to his country. Looking from the window, I knew that it was people who had mattered and what my mind most recalled was the sound of footsteps retreating for the last time down the spiral staircase. For me the place was full of ghosts and I was glad that I was not now at Malvern.

But looking from the east window, I could see the buildings beyond the College that were still T.R.E. and I knew that there would be other leaders and other visions. For me it was over, but I knew that young men remained who would be as able as any that had gone before; men who were willing to give their labours to the building up of our armed strength on which, at least in our time, peace in our land depends.

INDEX

INDEX